BREAKING GROUND

PLI
PRESS

PLI PRESS is Practising Law Institute's highly regarded publishing division. Our team of dedicated publishing and information professionals is committed to providing you the highest-quality analysis and practice guidance while keeping you updated on current legal developments.

Each year, **PLI PRESS** publishes more than 100 treatises, practice guides, books on lawyering skills, yearbooks, answer books, and journals—written and updated by leading practitioners in their respective practice areas, and edited and managed by our in-house legal editors. We also produce more than 200 Course Handbook titles annually, each corresponding to one of PLI's award-winning CLE programs.

QUESTIONS ABOUT THIS PUBLICATION?

If you have questions about updates to this publication, billing, or shipments, or would like information about our other products, please contact **PLI customer service** at info@pli.edu or at (800) 260-4PLI.

For any other questions or suggestions about this book, please contact the PLI Press **editorial department** at plipress@pli.edu.

For general information about Practising Law Institute, please visit **www.pli.edu**.

To view a full list of PLI Press publications, visit **www.pli.edu/plipress**.

Practising Law Institute • 1177 Avenue of the Americas • New York, NY 10036

BREAKING GROUND

How Successful Women Lawyers Build Thriving Practices

Deborah B. Farone

PLI Press • New York City
#440257

Legal Editor: Lori Wood

LCCN: 2025947012

ISBN: 978-1-4024-4832-4 (hardcover)
ISBN: 978-1-4024-4951-2 (softcover)

To every woman who ever doubted her ability to succeed, you already own the ruby slippers

and

To Dr. Egidio A. Farone, who believed in me and supported me throughout this journey

About the Author

Deborah Farone has had the unique opportunity to play a role in developing the best practices in legal marketing by working with some of the most respected and demanding professionals in the world. Her advisory practice focuses on helping professional services firms and individuals with their marketing strategy, personal branding, training and development and strategic planning. She often moderates and speaks at law firm and legal department retreats and workshops.

Deborah is also the author of the best-selling legal marketing book, *Best Practices in Law Firm Business Development and Marketing* (PLI 2019), a work based on more than sixty interviews with successful law firm leaders and marketers, general counsel, and innovators in the profession. She carved out a niche by distinguishing herself as the chief marketing officer of two of the world's most prestigious law firms, Cravath Swaine & Moore LLP and Debevoise & Plimpton LLP. Prior to entering the legal marketing profession, she refined her business development and communications skills by working at the global management consulting firm Towers Perrin, now Willis Towers Watson. Today, she works with law and other professional services firms around the world. Deborah speaks regularly at law schools, law firm partner retreats, corporate meetings and industry conferences.

Table of Contents

Acknowledgements

I want to thank my parents, Phyllis and Henry Brightman, who inspired me to write. I remember being a child staring up at my mom as she put on her makeup to go out with my father on a Saturday night. She was constantly in motion, but I knew that as she meticulously drew on her eyeliner, she would be in one spot, concentrating and looking in her mirror. I would begin to sing her the little songs I had made up that day. She never laughed or told me I was silly—instead, she would say, "You should write that down." I know both my parents hoped that one day I would write a book, and in many ways, they were the driving force behind this one.

A book doesn't just happen. It involves a publisher, editors, and (a lot of) support.

I am deeply grateful to the extraordinary people who generously shared their time and insights for this book. Some I had the privilege of knowing long before I conceived the idea of writing this, while others I came to know through introductions—or simply because I so admired their work and accomplishments that I reached out. Each of them gave with remarkable candor, allowing me to see not only their successes but also the challenges behind the curtain, reminding me that even the most impressive journeys are rarely seamless. Despite their already full and demanding lives, they carved out the time to share their stories, ideas, and lessons so that others might benefit. For their honesty, generosity, and spirit, I am profoundly thankful.

I would like to extend my special thanks to the individuals who contributed to the production of the book—most notably the brilliant and talented professionals at PLI. Lori Wood, my editor, has the patience and fortitude of both of the lions that frame the steps of the New York Public Library. Her guidance and judgement are impeccable, and her eye for detail is unmatched.

Thank you also to PLI's spectacular President Sharon Crane, and the superstar team of Kara O'Brien, David Smith, Alexa Robertson, Stephanie Sica, and Shaun Liboon for their incredible support and belief in the message conveyed in this book.

My friends who helped review the book were a tremendous help, including Diane O'Donnell, who is genuinely an editor in every sense of the word. You didn't miss your calling. It just came a little later than expected. And a big thank you to Terri Roth and Katrina Dewey, who took the time to read and review my manuscript.

On a personal note, I want to thank my husband, Egidio Farone, for his support and guidance—and for not laughing when we first met thirty-four years ago and I told him I was planning to write a book.

And to my family, a thank you to Rebecca Brightman and Bruce, Joshua and Samuel Altman; Raffaela, Christopher, Mia, and Malena DiStasio; and Josephine, Joseph, and Giovanna Tarulli. This has been a year of challenges as well as blessings.

To my amazing and supportive friends, especially Robin and Andy Stamelman, Linda Orton, JeanMarie Campbell, Nicole Petrie, Natalie Loeb, Susan Weinberger, Tim Armstrong, Jeffrey Klein, Margaret Nicholls, Allen Parker, Allan Schoenberg, Michael Williams, as well as the high school gang, Alison Frankel, Ilene Marquardt, Lisa Clifford, Irene Glemboski and Deborah Levy, thank you for sticking with me through this process. And a thank you to those others who are no longer here but whose presence is felt as I write this, my forever friends Cathy Saffer Stephenson and Anita Shapiro.

And to Mrs. Lucy Doberman—thank you for loyally staying by my side this past year, keeping me company, and making sure I stepped outside and into my garden a few times each day.

Introduction

Denise was an incredible lawyer. She was a fearless litigator who could stand up in court and, seemingly without notes, tear out the heart of any witness on the stand. She was also an intimidating manager. If you were an associate called into Denise's office, you had better be prepared to be a fiendish note-taker because, as Denise said, she "never suffered fools" and never wanted to repeat her requests to an associate. It was not a comfortable experience to be called to see Denise and be told to take a seat in one of her wingback guest chairs. You undoubtedly didn't want to ask her twice for additional details on an assignment. She was known around the firm for being extraordinarily tough.

Denise was the daughter of a world-famous inventor. While her brains and incredible work ethic may have been inherited, independently, she had developed a reputation for being a very serious and masterful lawyer.

Knowing all of this, I was surprised when one Friday afternoon, Denise called me into her office and asked me to take a seat. After a few uncomfortable moments waiting in one of those notorious wingbacks, she stared out the window and said, "I have a problem. I don't know how to get clients."

Her words shocked me. She turned to me and said quietly, almost in a whisper, "I have been getting most of my work from the firm's corporate lawyers and now that gravy train is about to stop." She explained that with other smart young litigators coming up in the ranks, the conveyor belt of referred cases she had grown to expect might be ending. It was then tears began to well up in her eyes, and she asked me, "Is it too late to learn how to develop business?"

It's because of Denise and other women partners and senior associates who have asked me over the past few years whether they have what it takes to develop a business, that I decided to write this book.

Two important things to know.

First, it's never too late to develop the skills necessary for rainmaking, and all of us, men and women, can become rainmakers. People have different styles and strengths, but every lawyer has the capability. It just needs to be developed and unleashed.

Second, what makes us as women different from men, besides biology, is that oftentimes we've not had the same exposure, training, or role models that many of our male counterparts have had in their business lives. We know that there are fewer women in management at law firms and even fewer leading those firms.

My own voyage in-house at law firms started at Debevoise & Plimpton, a wonderful international law firm, where I worked to establish and grow the firm's first marketing and business development department. It was in the very early days of legal marketing. I was then recruited by a team of M&A partners to join Cravath, a firm consistently revered as the country's most prestigious partnership. I spent years developing a strong business development and intelligence unit, an in-house public relations and internal communications team, and several other functions. After leaving Cravath, I began consulting with a number of law firms, but at the same time, I had an important project taking up a significant space in my head. I conducted interviews with law firm chairs, rainmakers, and other leaders in the profession in order to write *Best Practices in Law Firm Business Development and Marketing*, published by PLI in 2019.

My hope is that by sharing what I've learned, both from my own professional experiences and from the approximately sixty lawyers and other experts I interviewed for this book, that these pages can help others as they go on their marketing journey.

The book you are now reading is not about changing the bias or the inequity of the system. Those are things we need to continue to work hard to change. We need to speak out and continue to fight injustices and beliefs that harm diverse lawyers or others whose talent is overlooked. According to Decipher Investigative Intelligence, while women billed 6% more hours than men, men on average had a 14% higher billing rate. Are women perceived as having less expertise?

According to Julie Henson, Chief Growth Officer at Decipher, "Women partners in law firms are billing more—but being paid less, valued less, and credited less. Men hold the advantage in rates, originations, and client control—not because they work harder, but because the system still rewards legacy over merit. Until that changes, equity in law will remain a myth."

While we won't change bias today, this week or this month, one thing each of us can control is how we respond to those conditions and how we take the reins. By actively establishing our own reputations, building networks and creating practices, we can create our own paths to success.

Each of the following chapters provides many ideas and practical tips to apply to your own business development efforts. With this in mind, there are deep area experts in various fields, from social media to networking, who have great insights into what works when growing a practice and developing a reputation. I've reached out to some of them for their guidance, to test some hypotheses and to write the special "Think Pieces" that come at the end of each chapter.

I hope you will enjoy the book and find the material thought-provoking and helpful.

"Don't sit down and wait for the
opportunities to come. Get up and make them."

— Madam C.J. Walker (1867–1919),
first self-made female millionaire in the United States

Chapter 1

Why Is Business Development Different for Women?

"Independence is Happiness."

—Susan B. Anthony

Access Denied: The Missing Seat at the Table

A few years ago, at a local bar association meeting, a young African-American lawyer made her way up to me after a lecture. She said she wanted some advice. She relayed that while she loved being a lawyer and felt fortunate to be practicing law at a leading law firm, she was facing an issue. She wanted to learn how to develop business and had asked partners and the firm's business development department how she might get involved. But while she was often invited to attend pitch meetings, she felt she was never truly part of the pitch process.

The young lawyer knew that her firm bio, which included her portrait shot, was often included in new business pitches, regardless of whether she had substantive experience in the area the firm was pitching. Then if the written pitch was a success, and the firm was invited to the next stage to make an in-person presentation, she might be invited to the pitch meeting. Yet she was never given a speaking role. At the time I heard about this, I could only think that it was odd. As a CMO, I had been involved in hundreds of new business pitches, and my department was asked daily to prepare binders of pitch materials. While we might have worked with partners and associates to help them orchestrate and rehearse the pitch, we were not included in the meeting with prospects and rarely learned who had a speaking part.

The young lawyer also told me that if her firm was hired by the client for a legal matter, she might never be assigned to work on it. As she relayed her story, I could tell she was distraught by the situation. She said she didn't know what steps to take.

My initial advice to the young woman was to speak to her mentors at the firm and to those partners who had asked to include her bio in pitch materials or invited her to attend a meeting. Yet being that she was an associate, we both agreed that might be difficult. We discussed several other options, including speaking with the firm's HR department, but decided that if things didn't change at her current firm, she might want to consider moving to another firm.

This isn't just one female associate's story. It's a common story. And it points to a deeper, systemic issue.

Systemic Structures and Invisible Barriers

Laura Leopard, founder of Leopard Solutions, points out that the number of women partners has risen, but not dramatically. Today in the Am Law 200, the average percentage of women partners is 29.5% and less than a quarter of the Am Law 200 are led by women.

"It's a difficult barrier for many women to break through," Laura says. "I believe women simply don't receive the same opportunities as men in order to succeed. Instead, they have to break against their own cultural patterns and advocate for themselves."

Traditionally, law firms used to say that it was a pipeline, and there were just not enough women lawyers coming into the profession. We now know that it is no longer true. Women are choosing law school, and they are deciding to enter firms. According to the most recent NALP survey, women made up 51.62% of associates in 2024, the second time that women were a majority in the thirty-plus years that the NALP has been tracking firm diversity data.[1]

Despite the growing representation of women in the profession, in some situations, men in positions of leadership may be less comfortable asking women to join them in certain activities or possibly make assumptions based on gender. For example, a male partner might be less inclined to ask a female colleague to be his plus-one for a client lunch or to invite a woman to join the male partners at the firm's box for hockey games. While firms are changing, and many now have programs in place to address this disparity, it is still a challenge to reflect back to a practice leader or successful male rainmaker to show them their own biases. In many cases, this bias is not intentional, but bringing awareness to it is important.

The reality today can be a tough one. For many women, the biggest hurdle isn't ability—it's access. Too often, they're not in the room for those formative moments: the casual lunch with a client, the walk back from a meeting where insight is shared, or the pitch where a seasoned partner asks for the business. These moments are where business development is often learned—not in a classroom, but by watching and doing. Without regular exposure to these experiences or role models to mirror, it can be hard to figure out how to confidently step into the business-getting role. It's not

---

1. Nat'l Assoc. for Law Placement (NALP), 2024 Report on Diversity in U.S. Law Firms, https://www.nalp.org/uploads/Research/2024-25_NALPReportonDiversity.pdf.

about a lack of talent. It's about a lack of opportunity to see how it's done.

Firms are getting smart about this. Some firms now track who gets assigned to work on key client matters, and even further, many are looking at what type of work and what new skills those matters provide to associates. Other law firms have created unconscious bias programs, holding up a mirror to their lawyers and other professionals to show them how their approaches to those who don't look or sound like them limit the promise of the whole firm.

In addition, many Fortune 100 companies have been paying attention to diversity staffing at law firms. And more women and minorities now occupy in-house counsel positions and are responsible for helping select law firms. In such situations, while a diverse pitch team and the promise of a working group reflecting that team on the potential client's cases will not guarantee the firm wins the business, the complete lack of diversity might detract from the firm's appeal.

What the Research Tells Us

Women often face a higher bar to demonstrate credibility and earn the attention and respect of decision-makers, but can excel at understanding the client's business, putting the client's needs first, and reading nonverbal cues.

Scott Westfahl is the Director of Harvard Law School's Executive Education program and teaches courses on leadership, design thinking, and innovation within the school's J.D. curriculum. Before joining HLS, he served as Director of Professional Development at Goodwin Procter LLP, where he spent nearly a decade focusing on lawyer training and leadership development.

> "To engage in business development, you have to know what your value is and be able to communicate that confidently."
>
> **—Scott Westfahl**

Drawing from both research and practical experience, Scott underscores a persistent challenge in law firm culture: the disconnect between what is rewarded and how women are often socialized to behave. "Research shows women are less interested in self-promotion," he explains, noting that this creates a structural disadvantage in environments where visibility and self-advocacy lead to opportunity.

Scott links this issue back to the legal training pipeline itself, where law students are taught to focus on service and precision, not self-presentation. "To engage in business development, you have to know what your value is and be able to communicate that confidently," he says. Yet many women, trained to be excellent and modest, hesitate to assert themselves or claim credit. In contrast, men often leverage informal networks, visibility, and bolder self-advocacy to advance—sometimes regardless of comparative results. Scott warns that overlooking this dynamic isn't just a missed chance for women; it's a missed opportunity for firms to fully capitalize on their talent. "The challenge," he suggests, "is not just about encouraging women to promote themselves—but rethinking the environments that make self-promotion feel like a risk."

Catherine Zinn is Chief Client Officer at Baker Botts L.L.P. and a well-known advisor to companies involved in the technology sectors. Catherine was one of the first salespeople to enter the world of law firms when she left JAMS Mediation and Arbitration. It was at JAMS where she got to know a large cadre of lawyers.

She then went on to work at law firms, including DLA Piper and Orrick.

Throughout her career, Catherine has coached men and women within law firms, political organizations and corporations, including founders of start-ups. "I believe to this day, I don't know when and if it will change, that women have a higher bar for getting the attention of investors and other market influencers than men do. Women have to demonstrate credibility and work harder to earn respect and confidence of the decision-makers."

And the issues are the same around the world. During the process of writing this book, I spoke with women in North America, Africa, Asia and Europe. I heard over and over again that it is still a world in which most of the leaders are men.

Annalisa Reale is a leading labor and employment lawyer and a partner at the Italian law firm Chiomenti Studio Legale. She is fierce when it comes to advocating for her clients but also sees the nuance in making her way in a world not always set up for women.

Annalisa believes that it is still different for women, particularly in Italy and other parts of Europe. "We still live in a world that is populated mainly by men in business. We've been working a lot at it, not just women in law but in business in general and things are going better. But still, I don't believe we are there. So, when you sit in a board meeting or come on as an advisor in important meetings, you'll still find yourself to be the only one or just one of a few women at the table."

Leading with Authenticity: Real-World Advice

So how have successful women rainmakers thrived even when there has been insufficient training in business development available to them? Many of them have focused on doing great work and have not depended on law firms to help them get a leg up on the ladder. While formal training and firm support can be incredibly valuable, some women have simply created their own paths.

Roberta Downey is Head of International Construction at the law firm Vinson & Elkins, based in London, and an admired practitioner with thirty years of experience in commercial real estate disputes. Roberta strongly supports the women's initiatives at her firm—but warns against relying solely on that help and women-only events for business development. "I think there's a danger sometimes for young women to do all their business development in that women's category," she explains. "You are excluding half the population." Events focused exclusively on women may unintentionally limit access to broader client opportunities: "Whatever people say, few men feel comfortable going to a women's event."

Her core advice for women lawyers? Don't lead with diversity but rather lead with excellence. "You want them to give you a job because you're the best. 'They like me, and they trust me. And I happen to be a woman.'"

At the same time, Roberta encourages women to embrace what makes them stand out. "I stand out because I'm a woman," she says of working in the male-dominated construction industry. "It is much easier for me to build a profile and be more memorable." She even draws inspiration from the late Queen Elizabeth, who was known for wearing bright colors so she could stand out in a crowd. "Whereas the men all look like flight attendants on days off or bankers during the week, we as women can express ourselves through clothes and our hair, all of which makes us stand out from the crowd." Each time I meet with Roberta, she is wearing bright colors, such as shocking pink or bright yellow.

Roberta also stresses the importance of being attuned to family dynamics, both your own and your clients'. "Think like a woman," she advises. "If you know someone has small children, offer a lunch instead of a dinner. Afternoon tea instead of evening drinks. The client may not want to be out five nights a week."

Roberta sometimes invites clients and their spouses to opera performances and brings along her own partner to help make the evening feel social rather than transactional. "If the spouse of a client thinks, 'I really liked her,' that helps the relationship," she says. "It's not manipulative—it's thoughtful."

In sum, Roberta's message to women is both empowering and strategic: be visible, be smart, and be yourself. Roberta remarks, "Don't make gender the heart of your pitch."

Other women have been self-trained. They've picked up on ideas and nuance from the business world and then, consciously or subconsciously, created their own approach. Julie Spinelli, a partner at Le 16 Law in Paris, has built an international arbitration practice that would make any lawyer jealous. She is keenly aware of the gendered nuance in developing client relationships, especially when it comes to informal networking.

For example, while a casual drink with a potential male client might seem simple enough, for women it often comes with a set of unspoken calculations. "If you go for drinks with a prospective client," she explains, "you need to be very clear it's a business drink. Men don't have to think about this. For women, it's about how you behave, the table you choose, even the drink you order—just to make sure it remains professional."

This added layer of strategic self-monitoring and navigating optics while building rapport can feel exhausting. Julie notes that it's often easier to form comfortable relationships with other women simply because there's less second-guessing. "You're not as self-conscious and not as careful," she reflects.

Her experiences highlight a subtle yet persistent reality many women lawyers face: developing business while managing the risk of misinterpretation, especially in cross-cultural or male-dominated settings. It's one more example of how the business development playbook often needs editing, depending on who's holding it.

Karen Kahn EdD is a psychologist with a specialty in the psychology of gender difference and a senior coach who has been working exclusively with lawyers for twenty-five years. She believes that women may be neurologically wired for business development. "Women form connections among people and data. They're interrelated thinkers," she explains. "Men are more compartmentalized. That's just how we're built."

> "When you bring what you do naturally into business, you stop feeling like you're playing a role. And that's when clients start to really trust you."
>
> **—Karen Kahn**

For decades, however, women were taught to operate in a more transactional, masculine style because that's what traditional legal systems rewarded. But times have changed. "The marketplace has become more relational than transactional," Karen notes. "When women unplug from the skills they had to learn to survive in a masculine world, they have a step up." In her view, this is a prime moment for women to lead with empathy, connection, and authenticity—qualities that today's clients value most.

Karen encourages women lawyers to think of business development not as a chase but as cultivation—like growing a garden. "Going after business is aggressive and feels inauthentic for many women," she says. "But cultivating? That's about connection. That's something we do naturally." Rather than fearing rejection or trying to force "the ask," Karen reframes the process entirely. "The person with the most sustained, value-based relationships wins. Not the one who pushes hardest." She urges women to draw from what they already do every day—offering support, making introductions, checking in—not just because it feels better but because it works. "When you bring what you do naturally into business, you stop feeling like you're playing a role. And that's when clients start to really trust you."

Trust is something Marcia Hatch, a partner at Gunderson Dettmer Stough Villeneuve Franklin & Hachigian, LLP, knows well. She is a former college basketball player who seems to succeed at nearly everything she sets her mind to—including launching and building the firm's Ann Arbor, Michigan office, which she did ten years ago. Building trust with new clients was essential to her launching an office.

"It was about showing up, being authentic, and connecting on a personal level."

—Marcia Hatch

Marcia's approach to business development is as grounded and strategic as her game on the court once was—focused on consistency, connection, and playing the long game.

One of the most memorable stories she shared was from early in her career when she was invited to a low-key company barbecue hosted by a client's small team. Rather than showing up in formal lawyer mode, she brought her young children—and a kindergarten art project her son had worked on, featuring large letters filled with tiny woodland creatures. They gifted it to the CEO, who was so touched he framed the drawing and displayed it the board room. As Marcia put it, "It was about showing up, being authentic, and connecting on a personal level." That client remained loyal for years, continuing to refer business and even asking her to mentor his children.

Marcia's business development philosophy isn't about volume. It's about intentional, efficient relationship-building. "I wasn't great at big events," she shared. "I had to find a better approach." Instead of trying to network widely, she focused on deepening a handful of relationships by staying in touch at meaningful times, sending useful articles, and going the extra mile when it mattered. She also has a subtle but effective strategy for building mutual investment: asking for a small favor first. "If someone does something for you, it creates a little pattern of loyalty," she said. "That shared investment makes the relationship stronger—and more likely to last."

The women lawyers I've met are not lacking in talent or ability. They have an overabundance of skills. They found their own way of achieving great things.

As you will see, the women profiled in this book don't always mimic the traditional behavior of other lawyers. They succeed by building strong, authentic relationships—by leading with empathy, showing up consistently, and earning trust over time. And when women reframe business as offering value—not selling—they're able to show up with confidence and thrive.

Think Piece

Finding a Solution: i.WILL

By Andrea Markstrom*

For as long as I can remember, I have believed in the power of connection. I have seen, over and over again, that when women support one another, mentor one another, and open doors for one another, lives change. Careers grow. Entire communities rise.

Throughout my own professional journey, in an industry where leadership tables have often been dominated by men, I dreamed of creating a space where women could come together not just to network, but to truly lift each other up. I wanted to build something more than a group or a club, something that would inspire leadership and learning, and help every woman in the room realize her full potential.

That is what led me to create i.WILL, Inspiring Women Igniting Leadership and Learning.

By day, I serve as a Chief Information Officer, where I work closely with our Executive Committee to identify, plan, and implement technology and security solutions that align with the goals of the firm, our practice groups, and our business teams. I lead our

---

* Andrea Markstrom is the Chief Information Officer at Cadwalader, Wickersham & Taft LLP, guiding the firm's technology and cyber strategies to deliver innovative solutions and superior services. Andrea has over thirty years of leadership experience in global IT for law firms and large corporations. She is also the founder and CEO of i.WILL, a networking organization for career advancement. Her accolades include winning the New York CIO of the Year Orbie twice, the Woman of Influence in Legal Tech award, and the Woman in Cyber award from New York's ISACA Chapter. Andrea serves as Chair of Inspire CIO's NYC Chapter, mentors Northeastern's Technology MBA program, and holds board positions with several legal tech companies.

IT organization and ensure that we continue delivering superior technology services and support. I also bring more than thirty years of experience leading global information technology organizations for large law firms and corporations.

Along the way, I have often found myself as "the only," the only woman in the room, the only person in my role without a traditional background, or the only one willing to ask the hard questions. What I have learned is this: no one gets anywhere alone. We all rise faster, go further, and achieve more when we have a strong community behind us.

That is why I founded i.WILL, to give women across industries a space to connect, to learn, and to thrive.

And to be clear, i.WILL is not just another networking group or a one-time conference. It is a movement, a community built around three core pillars:

- *Creating Connections* through bi-monthly networking events and an annual all-day summit that combine leadership inspiration with professional development. These events are designed not just to work the room, but to foster authentic relationships and meaningful conversations.
- *Mentorship and Shared Learning* because mentorship has played such an important role in my own career. I wanted i.WILL to be a place where women can give and receive guidance, share lessons learned, and help one another grow. Our mentorship program is all about creating those personal connections that can open doors and change lives.
- *Giving Back* through our commitment to supporting nonprofits that help women and families succeed. We also fund women entrepreneurs through startup pitch competitions, because helping the next generation of business leaders is part of our mission.

The spirit of i.WILL is rooted in action. It is about turning conversations into commitments. It is about taking the inspiration we gain from one another and using it to drive real change in our companies, our communities, and in ourselves.[1]

1. For more information about joining i.WILL, you can contact Andrea at info@i-will.net or andrea@i-will.net.

Chapter 2

Building and Promoting Your Profile

"The best protection a woman can have . . . is courage."

—Elizabeth Cady Stanton

When I was a marketing major in college, one of my professors gave us an assignment that I will always remember: Create a full-scale marketing campaign to sell disposable razors. The core challenge was to address how to differentiate our fictitious client's razor from all the other razors on the market, during a time when all razors looked and worked pretty much the same way. The professor explained that these products were parity products: competitive products that might have tiny differences but features so minutely different from one another that a consumer might not be able to tell them apart. They were somewhat interchangeable, and as with most parity products, there was less likelihood that a consumer of disposable razors would be brand loyal.

The accepted thinking was that a consumer walking into a drugstore would easily choose the least expensive version or select the brand that was easiest to reach on the shelf. Getting a consumer to change from one parity product to another, particularly when they weren't unhappy with the razor they currently used, could also be a difficult challenge. Marketing a parity product was not a simple assignment.

So how could we find a way to create something different, when the competition's product was very much the same? One group of classmates suggested changing the product slightly, by offering different color razors. Others said that a stunningly creative ad campaign could help demonstrate the razor in a different light or target a different demographic. Another group suggested that we focus on one of the attributes, such as super-strong razor blades, even though the other razors had the same blades. In the end, we learned that selling a parity product was complex, and took a deep understanding of the market, and a very clear idea of the product's position in the marketplace. We also needed to focus on the consumer and the features and benefits that mattered most to them.

Lawyers are not consumer products one finds on a drugstore shelf, and certainly not all lawyers are of the same caliber, but there is a cloud of parity in how clients often view their lawyers and law firms. While there are firms with stellar reputations in specific practice areas, it's often difficult to tell them apart from the outside. And as we know with trends in the lateral market, lawyers often switch to new firms, only to be replaced by a new set of lawyers. According to Decipher Investigative Intelligence, five years after a lateral moves to a law firm (in this case, one of the National Law Journal 500), 45%–62% of those lawyers will leave the firm.[1]

When that happens, as it does quite often today, clients may perceive lawyers as more fungible, and easy to replace. Add to that the fact that many law firms are hard to differentiate solely based on their marketing and overall brand. There are several reasons, particularly price, that lead to clients having less loyalty to a firm brand.

---

1. Decipher Investigative Intelligence and ALM Legal Intelligence, Risky Business: Rethinking Lateral Hiring (2022).

One way a firm might differentiate itself is when it notices patterns or trends in the marketplace and remains flexible to make shifts in its practice. Another way is to see if there are missing niches that might be filled.

Knowing What Makes You Different

After establishing herself as a standout mergers and acquisitions lawyer in India's elite legal circles, Tahera Mandviwala, a qualified solicitor in India, England and Wales, and the United States, recognized a gap in the India market that few others had noticed. There was no fully comprehensive and completely dedicated private client practice serving high-net-worth individuals across India. Despite her success at her firm, TDT Legal, and her visibility in corporate law, she took a bold and risky step. Tahera pivoted from a comfortable position to build a new practice area from the ground up. She didn't want to be considered one of the many in a large group of M&A lawyers based in India but rather as someone with a unique set of skills that could be provided, in a streamlined way, to a specific group of clients. In her case, she aimed at private high-net-worth clients.

It was a move that required not just stretching her legal acumen but exercising her entrepreneurial vision. "I was very happy in my M&A practice. I was great there," she said. "It would've taken a lot to budge me out of it. But the more I looked into it, the more I realized, 'Let's take the risk.'" Tahera reeducated herself, built a team, trained them, and raised awareness of the value of private client work—both among clients who didn't know they needed it and peers who hadn't yet seen it as a distinct area of expertise.

> "In a country with two million lawyers, you need to find your niche."
> **—Tahera Mandviwala**

A decade later, her firm is recognized as a market leader in this space. "In a country with two million lawyers, you need to find your niche," she said. "And I was lucky. It was an entire practice area." Tahera's decision not only distinguished her professionally but also created an enduring platform for cross-selling, client retention, and market leadership.

She no longer has to explain her value. Referrals and repeat work come to Tahera because she's known as the go-to lawyer in the field of private client work.

Creating a Niche

So how else can you create a niche and differentiate yourself from the crowd?

While it's useful to examine how other people have positioned themselves and to think about what works for them in the market, that's only a small part of the equation. The most important element in considering how to differentiate yourself is to look at your own strengths.

You may be the most brilliant lawyer with the most glowing credentials, yet if you are unable to clearly articulate what sets you apart, you will have a hard time developing business in a competitive market. Without the specificity for the types of legal issues you handle and the particular industry in which you have knowledge, you are less likely to build a robust practice. When I speak at law firm retreats, I often ask partners to turn to the person next to them and introduce themselves as if they were at a cocktail party, speaking with a businessperson who is not a lawyer. Most often, they have trouble finding the right words or narrowing down their focus. The point is that only once you have clarity about what you are selling can you begin to market yourself effectively.

> "You don't get business by hoping someone notices your brilliance."
>
> **—Heather Nevitt**

"You don't get business by hoping someone notices your brilliance," said Heather Nevitt, Editor-in-Chief of *Corporate Counsel* at ALM and a leading voice in the legal industry. A lawyer by training and now a journalist and in-demand speaker, Heather helps lead the popular Women, Influence & Power in Law (WIPL) program. Heather has spent her career examining both the practice and the business of law. "For a long time, I thought if I just did excellent work, that would be enough. I thought someone would say, 'Wow, she's great. We should give her more.' But it doesn't work like that." Like many women who begin their careers heads-down and focused on delivering results, she learned that rainmaking isn't a reward for good behavior—it's a skill set all its own.

Heather described the mindset shift as both uncomfortable and empowering. "I had to rewire my thinking. I had to learn to follow up, to speak up, to say, 'I'd love to work with you on that.' It didn't always come naturally, but it made all the difference. You don't have to be aggressive. But you do have to be clear."

It's that clarity of purpose that matters, not only in how you market, but in giving you the confidence that is so vital to rainmaking.

It also helps you decide what type of law you want to practice and how you will create your career.

Heather's perspective—shaped by years practicing law and now advising and interviewing the industry's top minds—underscores a powerful truth: The path to building influence and a book of business starts with making your value visible, both to yourself and to others.

Of course, in order to know your value, you must have a clear perspective on your niche, and how you want to be known.

Think of the rainmakers you know, or the top business generators in your firm. They are often known as experts in a particular area. For example, Carol is a litigator who handles financial fraud cases, or Bob is an M&A lawyer who works with mid-market companies. While there may be several things that you are capable of doing or at which you excel, it helps to home in and create a strong practice-oriented niche for yourself.

Introspection is not always easy, but here are two exercises to help you focus on your niche. The first is a list of questions to consider. I generally advise clients to keep a pad of paper or a notebook, dedicated to business development ideas and prospects. The notebook often begins with a page with their answers to these questions.

Exercise 1: Thinking About Your Niche

What will make me happy?

- What brings me the most joy in my work?
- Which matters or cases have I found most fulfilling?
- What aspects of my work do I dread? (It's important to know this. While you may be thought of as great in M&A, if term sheets and detailed agreements make you turn green, it may not be the right area for you.)

Is there a business need for this practice?

- Where is there demand for what I do?
- What industries or sectors are growing or underserved?
- Will this niche help me build a sustainable, profitable practice?
- Are there upcoming regulations, market trends, or business shifts that could create future demand?

How does this fit with my current firm's work?

- Does this niche fit within my firm's broader practice areas?
- Could the firm's client conflicts limit my ability to pursue this niche?
- Does this area offer opportunities to cross-sell within the firm?

Another simple exercise I've used with clients is to work with them on creating a Venn diagram.

Exercise 2: A Niche Venn Diagram

Draw a Venn diagram, with overlapping circles. One circle represents the things that you love to do that you are good at doing. Think about the various types of matters that you've enjoyed the most. The second circle is the need in the marketplace for particular help in an industry or type of problem. Finding that sweet spot, where there is an overlap between what you love to do and where there is a market need is where you can often begin to narrow in on finding a niche. The best niche is the one that combines doing the work that you love with a need in the marketplace.

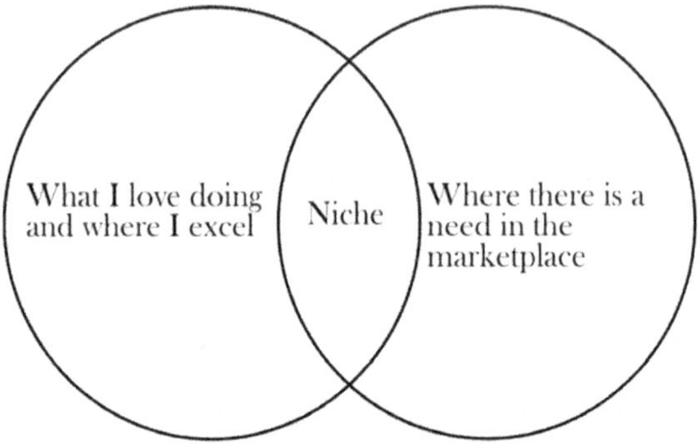

Once you do find a niche to pursue, apply some reverse engineering. Think about the attributes and accomplishments that you have that help you differentiate yourself.

Is it that you've tried a certain number of cases regarding that topic? Is it that you've represented XYZ company as they faced the toughest matter of their existence? Is it that you've had experience outside of a law firm that is particularly relevant?

Think like a litigator building a case. What are those few things that help differentiate you from the lawyer down the hall? What makes you special? What makes you not a parity product? Be able to articulate those features of your experience and practice.

With the competitive landscape, and the view of in-house counsel that lawyers seem fungible, it's important to create a niche and to stand out. If you are fortunate to be at a firm with a marketing department, chances are they will work on promoting and differentiating the brand of the firm. If they have the appropriate staff, they may also support you in helping you refine and market your niche. Yet, ultimately, you are the one who makes the decision to have a personal niche, one that fits with the firm's ethos, and gives you enough of a position to stand out in the world.

Without a clear niche, it's harder to figure out what types of marketing to do, how to proactively gain clients, and how to cross-sell within your firm. Creating a niche and knowing your position within a marketplace is the first step in any type of personal brand building.

Personal brand is the intersection of how you want to be seen and how others see you. To have a strong, positive personal brand requires that you be very intentional about how people see you. Consistency in your own messaging will help. Without it, you may be perceived as just another lawyer, off the shelf.

Keep Your Niche Front of Mind, the Right Way

Early in her career, lawyer Roberta Downey of Vinson & Elkins asked herself a question that shaped much of her marketing approach: "How do I make sure my name stays front of mind, in a good way?" Much of Roberta's work involves working around the globe, providing bespoke attention to the complexities of large-scale, cross-border construction projects.

One of the answers that she came up with was to create a construction-themed desk calendar that she sends to clients each year featuring the projects she has worked on with them and others over the past year. "The beauty about a calendar is that our clients have it on their desk all year round," she says. It's tangible, personal, and effective. It reminds people exactly of who Vinson & Elkins is and reminds them of her team's talent.

Another way she stays front of mind is through writing handwritten notes. "There's something quite visceral about seeing somebody's handwriting." Whether through handwritten cards, calendars or the occasional invitation to an event, Roberta has created meaningful, low-pressure ways to stay visible and valued, in a way that feels comfortable and authentic.

Authentic Promotion

"Good, better, best, never let it rest, until the good is better and the better is the best." This is an old saying that my mom used to repeat to me and to my sister when we were young, to encourage us to always do our best.

The problem, as Heather Nevitt pointed out, is that even though many of us may do our best, we don't always get the promotion, win the client or capture the attention we deserve. One ingredient that is often missing in the mix is the need to promote your work and find what makes you unique.

Promoting oneself, particularly as a woman, used to be seen as unseemly, and it has also been viewed as being unfeminine. The best technical phrase I can use in addressing that concern is, we need to get over it. I know that is easier said than done, but you can promote yourself in a way that is befitting of you. There is no one-size fits-all plan for doing this, but it's essential to find the authentic steps that work for you.

Jami McKeon is the Chair of legal powerhouse Morgan Lewis, where she has served in the role for more than a decade. She is a legend in the business and a role model for all genders. Jami is known for spearheading the firm's global growth and transforming the firm into a global powerhouse with 2,200 lawyers across thirty-three offices worldwide.

Jami believes that one of the most overlooked keys to business development is authenticity. While law firms often try to identify the "ideal rainmaker profile," Jami makes it clear that there is no single mold. "You can have someone who's incredibly introverted and not very sociable who's a great business developer," she noted, "and sometimes you have somebody who seems like they're really sociable who doesn't do as well." The through-line isn't personality type. As Jami points out, instead, it's a genuine dedication to the client's needs and a consistent, credible presence.

"You have to be authentically you.
You can never be more than second best
at trying to be someone else."

—Jami McKeon

As she puts it, "You have to be authentically you. You can never be more than second best at trying to be someone else."

Authenticity, she explains, is what allows lawyers to build real trust, and trust is what drives business. "What clients really need is someone who inspires confidence. You need to be practical, thoughtful, creative, and deeply understand what the client is trying to achieve." Rather than focus on style, she encourages lawyers to develop substance: being able to listen, synthesize, and offer meaningful solutions. "Clients want more than legal knowledge. They want someone who can extract the issues, respond efficiently, and truly add value. And you can't do that if you're pretending to be someone else."

All sides of the globe echo the concept that clients want and expect more than simple legal know-how. They want bespoke work, real relationships and to be acknowledged in an authentic way. This is echoed from clients as well as from the consulting side of the legal ecosystem, from those who have experienced and worked with thousands of lawyers.

Helen Burness is a leader in the legal social media marketing area and founder of Saltmarsh Marketing. Helen is based in the United Kingdom but is a must-follow for anyone on the planet when it comes to learning how to use social media. She also challenges one of the most persistent myths in law.

Helen says, "There's this legacy thinking that if you're a good lawyer, people will find you. But it's not true anymore. The world is noisy. The market is noisy. And clients have choices."

She notes that many lawyers don't make their value clear, both in person and especially online. "When I train lawyers on LinkedIn, I say that you need to clearly say who you are, what you do, and who you do it for. Otherwise, even your closest contacts won't know how to refer work to you."

As Helen points out, you also need to know your values. What do you stand for? What issues do you think are important, that maybe sit aside from your day-to-day work, but touch the business world? Sustainability, leadership, diversity and inclusion? Share views that will connect you with others beyond being a lawyer.

Helen talks about the need to move away from leaving a trail of hopeful breadcrumbs that someone will follow. "We inhabit a world that is so digitally noisy, it is important to make it as easy as possible for someone to see who you are, what you do and how they might be able to work with you." Helen advises, "Create a trail that leads somewhere. Make it easy for someone to say, 'They're the person I need to call for that issue.' It's not about being loud, it's about being unmistakable."

Authentic Relationships

Mary Wilson at Dentons credits her success to consistent, relationship-driven networking—particularly with peers early in her career. Mary is Denton's US Managing Partner and serves on the firm's U.S. and global boards. She is a national finance, healthcare and tax-exempt organizations lawyer.

How did Mary get her business and build her profile? Most of it started by knowing her niche and building connections within the firm. Encouraged by a rainmaking mentor, Mary focused on getting to know clients and fellow firm lawyers during her work travel to different cities.

She also did something other superstar rainmakers have done. She understood that building a profile and building relationships starts early. She worked on developing her niche, and at the same time, maintained relationships with peers at her level across investment banks, other law firms, and commercial banks. Over time, those friendships became referral sources.

"Nobody is so amazing that their entire book of business is generated by themselves," Mary said. One story that illustrates her philosophy: She recently took a former mentor to lunch just to thank him for his support, only to have him later refer her to a major new client. "I did not arrange for that lunch to get work," she emphasized, "but it was a reminder of the power of networking."

Building Your Profile

In case there is any doubt, increasing your profile can do several things:

- You will add credibility and credential yourself in your arena of practice.
- You will become better known and more likely to get the call for a new client, speaking opportunity or promotion.
- You will start to mirror back and believe in yourself today, a bit more than you did yesterday.
- You will be more likely to attract the type of work that you enjoy and that brings you fulfillment.

So now that you know what it is that makes you unique, it's time to share it with the outside world.

In PR, there is a saying that "press begets press." The same is true of building a strong professional reputation: Once you have it, it becomes easier to both attract and pursue new opportunities.

When preparing to meet with a client, you gather information to deliver a targeted, persuasive presentation. But remember—if you're at the stage where you're being considered for an assignment, the potential client is also checking you out. Consider what they'll see when they search for your name online. If you don't consciously create a profile, you will still have one—one in which you've ceded control.

If you introduce yourself to a potential client, having a reputation—perhaps from articles about you or from a talk you gave—can make them more comfortable and receptive to hiring you. Should you decide to switch jobs, your strong, positive personal brand will make it more likely that you'll land an interview. A robust profile in a particular area also increases the chances of being offered speaking engagements, media interviews, and other valuable opportunities. In many ways, developing a niche and reinforcing it with colleagues and the outside world is building an asset. Like any valuable asset, creating a niche and developing a profile need regular attention and care to grow and thrive. When done well, your profile can work for you, opening doors to opportunities you might never have known about otherwise.

Imposter Syndrome

Clare Grossman is the Director of Development at National Association of Minority & Women Owned Law Firms (NAMWOLF). Clare describes the membership as thriving, driven, and business-savvy. She points out, "These women know they must develop business to survive—there's no room for hesitation when payroll is due."

Even among these women, however, Clare sees that imposter syndrome is real. Imposter syndrome surfaces as a major, resonant issue, especially for younger women lawyers in male-dominated firms. "It's described as more than just self-doubt; it's a catchall for feeling out of place in environments where the top leadership and power structures remain largely male. The conversation hints at a deeper need for inclusive role models and supportive cultures that go beyond checking boxes." Yet through it all, these women are networking, creating personal profiles and marketing their practices.

Sara Koleilat-Aranjo brings a uniquely global perspective to her legal practice, shaped by a life and career spent in Saudi Arabia,

Lebanon, France, the United Kingdom, the United States, and the United Arab Emirates. Born in Riyadh to a French Lebanese family, she was educated in the French system, earned multiple master's degrees, practiced law in Paris and London, and is now based in Dubai, where she leads the regional litigation and arbitration practice and serves as global head of arbitration for her firm.

Despite her many achievements, Sara still experiences imposter syndrome. "Let's be honest, many lawyers, predominantly women, suffer from it. I still have it. But I've learned to manage it better." She recalled the nervousness she felt before her first major IBA panel appearance: "I remember the growing sense of disbelief and telling myself, 'Why did I get myself into this?'" But the experience was fantastic, and it taught her something important: You don't have to wait until you feel ready to show up and do the work.

We discuss more about speaking engagements in a later chapter, but I leave you with Sara's advice. "Be brave, believe in yourself and seize opportunities," she said. "Even if you're not sure you're fully ready for it."

Think Piece

Building Communities That Build You: A Personal Journey from Outsider to Community Builder

By Priya Lele*

As Co-Founder & Chair of She Breaks the Law, I've established and lead a global network of women leaders and change makers (aka #lawbreakers[1]) who are driving change through innovation, inclusion, and collaboration. When my two co-founders and I launched She Breaks the Law six years ago, we never thought we'd grow into this global community of nearly 4,000 members from 50+ countries. Here are my reflections on what I've learned along the journey and why I believe building communities can raise a collective profile—not just for the community, but for those who champion it.

---

* Priya Lele is Co-Founder & Chair of She Breaks the Law, a global network of women leaders driving change in the legal ecosystem. With over two decades bridging traditional legal practice and digital innovation, she has held transformation leadership roles at EY, global law firms, and worked with several corporate legal departments across the United Kingdom, United States, EMEA, and Australia. A recognized thought leader and frequent international speaker on legal technology and diversity, Priya has received the European Women of Legal Tech Award (2020) and ILTA's Influential Women in Legal Tech (2025) and is passionate about creating inclusive pathways for women's leadership in law and technology.

1. An endearing term coined by us for women leaders who are challenging the norm, breaking the mold and innovating and disrupting our legal ecosystem—we are breaking the law for the better—together!

From Fighting My Way in Law to Building My Own Table

My story begins with a paradox: I was born into a legal family yet had to fight my way into the profession. My father, a lawyer himself, opposed me. "Law isn't a women-friendly profession," he'd say, genuinely believing it.

Born a rebel, I fought my way into law!

As a woman charting my own path, I often felt alone, even an "outsider"—coming from a small town in India to studying at Cambridge and working in Big Law, shifting from traditional legal practice into innovation roles, moving between countries and continents. I've often broken the mold and found myself in rooms I thought I didn't belong in.

She Breaks the Law grew from that need—to create a community where everyone "belongs"—a space where women from across the legal ecosystem could find their tribe, share authentically, and support each other through transitions and transformations.

It was also that long-held desire to prove my dad wrong and make law more women-friendly. When I met my co-founders—who shared my values—it was as if the stars were aligned. A chance meeting at the end of an innovation conference in London became a meeting of minds and hearts leading us to launch She Breaks the Law.

A Movement Is Born

I still remember sitting at my kitchen table on the eve of International Women's Day 2019, wrestling with excitement and doubt as we prepared to launch. As we watched the community grow in the first twenty-four hours from three to 125 members, we knew we were onto something—we'd touched the hearts of other like-minded women.

Six years on, we're a powerful platform for women leadership—connecting nearly 4,000 members across 50+ countries, and providing safe spaces to share, learn and grow together. We've developed specialized initiatives like Women in Legal AI, led first-of-its-kind, gender-lensed research on AI in law, and published an influential report "No Woman Left Behind—Closing the AI Gender Gap in Law" in partnership with Next 100 Years and Linklaters.

Our members regularly collaborate on or refer opportunities, find speakers for events, and some have even started their own niche networks. Every time I witness a women lawyer find her next opportunity or advance their career through connection—I'm proud of the organic professional development that happens through the community.

Living By Our Mottos

Two philosophies have guided everything we've built.

"Alone we can do so little, together we can do so much."

—Helen Keller

This ultimate lawbreaker beautifully captures the spirit of She Breaks the Law. By collaborating with her teacher, she broke the laws of society and limitation to become the first deaf-blind person to earn a Bachelor of Arts.

We co-founded She Breaks the Law to unite women across disciplines, backgrounds and geographies—breaking down silos and facilitating collaboration—to accelerate change and build a more inclusive and progressive legal ecosystem.

"We rise by lifting others."

—Robert Ingersoll

Our SheShares initiative exemplifies this. We deliberately seek out both well-known figures and unsung heroes, bringing authentic stories to light. It's not just the highlight reel—they share their struggles, doubts, and lightbulb moments that sparked change.

When we spotlight women, they gain visibility and credibility while providing roadmaps for others. Everyone benefits—the women sharing their stories, the women learning from them, and the community that grows stronger through these connections.

The Power of Community Amplification

These philosophies have shaped how we've built our global community—amplifying our collective efforts through connection, knowledge exchange, mentoring, and professional growth.

For our sixth anniversary this year, we launched a Change-Makers campaign, recognizing six extraordinary women across five continents whose initiatives have collectively impacted over half a million lives. Rather than focusing on us, we spotlighted other women accelerating action for gender equity in the legal ecosystem.

One of our six change-makers started WhatsApp groups in the UAE connecting 450+ women across five networks, facilitating job placements and mentorship. Another created a specialized M&A community in London where members generated nearly half-million pounds in referral revenue in its first year, with 69% reporting increased business development opportunities.

The Accidental "Personal" Discovery: Your Profile Isn't Built, It Emerges

What I hadn't realized while building the community, connecting others, and shining a light on inspiring women was that this would raise my own profile!

The network effect is real—every woman you help succeed remembers you. Every community member whose story you amplify becomes part of your professional narrative. Your credibility grows through association with meaningful impact. By consistently amplifying others' achievements, you become known as a connector and leader in the space.

The most powerful professional profile isn't one you build for yourself—it's one that emerges from the value you create for others!

I'm proud of my recent recognitions (e.g., the European Women of Legal Tech Award (2020) and ILTA's 2025 Influential Women in Legal Tech) because they celebrate the collective impact created, not just my individual professional contribution.

Building Each Other Builds Us All

When we women support and amplify one another, it naturally enhances our own visibility and credibility—and as you grow so does the power of your network. When you build a community with purpose and lead through values, recognition follows naturally, and your profile becomes the natural byproduct of meaningful impact.

"We rise by lifting others" isn't just a great philosophy; you lift an ecosystem—and it lifts you back.

Chapter 3

Creating and Disseminating Thought Leadership to Promote Your Expertise

"Unless I am allowed to tell the story of my life in my way, I cannot tell it at all."

—Mary Jane Seacole

In a world where voices compete for attention, owning your narrative has never been more crucial, especially for women lawyers striving to stand out in a crowded field. Thought leadership offers a powerful avenue to do just that. Through authentic storytelling, sharing insights, and demonstrating expertise, rainmakers have raised their profile, while cultivating trust and credibility within their networks. There are many ways of offering thought leadership. Webinars, podcasts, article writing, and white papers immediately come to mind. And LinkedIn, with its global reach and professional focus, has emerged as one of the ideal platforms for telling this narrative.

Thought leadership, combined with the strategic use of social media, can help all lawyers take control of their personal and professional narratives. By harnessing these easy-to-use tools (with very little or no expense), you can build a visible and meaningful presence and foster connections that propel successful business development.

The Value of Thought Leadership

Bobby Umar, a social media expert, was once one of the brains behind the Dove Campaign for Real Beauty (which I loved). The campaign showed women of all shapes and sizes feeling good about themselves. It offered up to those of us in marketing a good lesson about promoting values. "We weren't even selling product—we were selling the idea of real beauty and fostering positive self-esteem in young girls," he recalled.

What does selling soap have to do with selling legal expertise? Bobby sees a strong parallel between that campaign and how lawyers can market themselves—not solely by listing credentials, but by sharing the value they provide. Instead of saying "hire me," Bobby says "Lawyers should consider showing how they think, how they help, and how they serve. That's what will build a lasting connection."

Having an established profile beyond one's firm is not just helpful—it's essential. For lawyers, it can be a powerful way to build a reputation, create new opportunities, and deepen relationships.

Building a public profile through thought leadership has incredible value beyond marketing implications. Having a positive profile prepares lawyers for unexpected challenges—whether it's a career shift, economic downturn, or personal setback—because if it's done right, it gives a lawyer a network and reputation to lean on.

Bobby underscores the importance of clarity and intention when advising professionals who are just starting out. Similar to considerations when building a niche, Bobby recommends beginning with a defined objective: What kind of life, brand and thought leadership do you want to have? From there, he suggests optimizing your LinkedIn profile, creating a simple content strategy, and reaching out to people to start meaningful conversations. These early steps lay the groundwork for building influence and credibility professionally, especially for those in traditionally cautious fields like law.

Creating Useful and Authentic Thought Leadership

The Canadian philosopher Marshall McLuhan looked at forms of new media and famously said, "The medium is the message." Today, that's not the whole truth. Appearing on social media to share your honors, awards, and content you create is important, yet it's what you say, not just where you say it, that is significant.

Helen Burness, the U.K.-based marketing consultant, believes many lawyers confuse thought leadership with what she calls "marketing fluff." According to Helen, "Audiences using these tools don't want more self-promotion. They want perspective. They want to hear something that makes them think differently or helps them do their job better." True thought leadership, she says, requires taking a position. "You have to have a view. You have to be willing to ruffle feathers sometimes."

> "You have to have a view. You have to be willing to ruffle feathers sometimes."
>
> **—Helen Burness**

We often overlook something important: personality. So much of the legal content out there feels like it was produced by the same machine, just churned out with no soul. But the people we remember for their thought leadership, the ones who stand out, are the ones who let a bit of themselves shine through. Whether it's their personal story, tone, or humor, that's what makes them memorable. That's what builds a brand.

The truth is that the most powerful kind of profile-building isn't about trying to appear perfect. It's about being real, providing value and making an impression that sticks.

Some of the keys that drive success, particularly on social media, come from being useful and adding value to people with similar interests. As the algorithms behind LinkedIn and other types of social media show content to people with similar interests, you are much more likely to get additional audience members paying attention to your content when you write about something specific to their concerns. As for memorability and time spent on a post, those are also improved by providing helpful content.

Once you begin to create content, it can be useful and interesting to pay attention to the metrics of how many people viewed a post, or specifically where the views came from. Still, for those just starting out, don't pay too much attention to the numbers—consistency is the key. At a later time, metrics may help you assess how a post performed and what types of your posts do the best, but that can wait until you've built up a bank of content.

The Tools

Nicole Petrie is a highly regarded leader in professional service marketing and business development, with a career spanning law, consulting, and accounting firms. Today, she serves as the Chief Marketing and Business Development Officer at Proskauer. In her work with law firms, Nicole brings a strategic, growth-focused approach, partnering with lawyers to drive both brand and business outcomes. She has seen the tremendous value of using a tailored mix of tools—from social media and speaking engagements to webinars and client events—to raise visibility, build personal brands, and deepen client relationships. For Nicole, success lies not in doing everything but in doing the right things—intentionally and in alignment with business goals.

> "We're seeing a shift toward more humanizing content. People want to know who you are, not just what you do."
>
> **—Nicole Petrie**

Nicole views LinkedIn as an especially powerful platform. "It's a low-cost, high-impact way to share insights, show your personality, and stay top-of-mind with your network," she says. Nicole encourages lawyers to use social media in an authentic and engaging way. "We're seeing a shift toward more humanizing content. People want to know who you are, not just what you do," she adds.

When helping lawyers shape their outreach plans, Nicole begins with the business. "Like any planning process, you have to start with your vision and goals. Who are your key clients or prospects? Once you know that, you can determine whether social, speaking, or other tactics best support your thought leadership and growth priorities." For Nicole, effective marketing and business development is about focus—not frenzy.

Thought leadership isn't just about the written word, it can also mean appearing on a webinar, participating in a podcast, or using social media. The key is to think about your intended audience and which vehicle makes the most sense for reaching them. Just as important, though, is choosing a format that plays to your strengths. Marketing tends to work best when you do the things you enjoy, because those are often the areas where you excel.

Utilizing Bylined Articles

Bylined articles, articles where you are the author or a co-author with another professional, can be very helpful in cementing your reputation and establishing your professional credibility. By providing written longer-form content for your clients and prospects, you can share your knowledge and demonstrate how you think.

When considering writing a bylined article, there are questions to ask. First, consider what topic you want to cover and if it's one that is relevant to what makes you unique. Is this a topic where you feel you can add extra value to the discussion? Is this a topic where you would want to handle that kind of business if you were to get it? Is it the type of business that would be profitable and not cause conflicts for your firm?

Also, it's important to know what the publication's stance is on reprint rights. In the most favorable agreements, you'll hold the copyright and retain the right to reprint the article on your website and use it as you wish in other promotional efforts.

These are all questions to consider prior to jumping in and writing an article.

In the past, most lawyers saw publishing as the act of writing very long treatises, but today we often see requests for pieces between 800 and 1,000 words, generally one or two pages of text. Today's publications expect shorter articles that provide tangible, real-world advice.

Keep in mind your audience and what they need to know. While you won't be able to answer every question readers may have on the topic, part of the reason to write the article is to let them know that your topic is a complex subject, and if they need help, you are an expert in the area.

Getting Your Article Out into the World

Once a lawyer spends the hours to write a bylined article, and it has been published, it makes sense to consider how to "merchandise" the piece, by devising ways to repurpose it for other uses. Having checked on the reprint rights with the original publisher beforehand, you'll know how you can use the article after it appears in the publication.

Public relations professionals often use the term "campaign marketing" when referring to this approach. By selecting an issue you care about and ensuring it makes commercial sense to discuss, you can then consider how an article might be utilized for other uses.

Once you write an article, consider the various ways you can promote it. Here are just a few.

1. *Share on LinkedIn*: Post the article link on your feed with a brief, engaging summary or insight to draw attention. Consider tagging relevant people or organizations and using three to five relevant hashtags. If your piece has already appeared on LinkedIn, consider reposting it to other groups on LinkedIn to which you belong, such as associations or alumni networks.
2. *Send to key clients*: Email the article to select clients and prospects who might find it valuable, with a note highlighting why it's relevant to them.
3. *Post on your firm's website*: Ensure the article is added to the firm's website or blog, preferably with an author bio and a clear call to action (e.g., "Contact me to discuss . . .").
4. *Use in conference and speaking materials*: Incorporate the article into slides, handouts, or reference materials for relevant speaking engagements, webinars, or client seminars.
5. *Utilize for internal promotion*: Share the article internally within the firm to inform colleagues of your expertise and create opportunities for cross-selling or collaboration.

6. *Distribute to referral sources*: Send the article to trusted referral sources and business partners who might share it with their networks or recommend you to clients.
7. *Submit to relevant publications and associations*: For wider distribution and added credibility, submit the article to relevant legal or industry publications, newsletters, or professional associations.
8. *Reuse and recycle the content*: Break the article into shorter pieces for LinkedIn posts, client alerts, or even podcast or video scripts. You can also expand on the topic in a future article or series.

In many ways, you may want to think about this as a larger campaign around a certain issue. For example, if I were a lawyer interested in writing about a particular change in the law, I might write a bylined article. Then I might give a speaking engagement or host a webinar based on the messaging. After that, I might take the piece and send it to clients with a note asking if I could come in with my team to make a presentation. Much like a political campaign, a marketing campaign regarding a particular topic is multifaceted. It may take several approaches to get the information out to the audience you intend to reach. The steps may take place over a week, or several months, to draw attention to the issue.

Speaking engagements can also be vital in getting your thought leadership out into the ether. By personally delivering your message, you create more of a personal connection than you would through an article. If handled correctly, speaking engagements can have many other ancillary benefits, which will be discussed in another chapter.

The key to using all of these tools is to start off by thinking about the message or news you want to convey, ensure it makes sense to write about it, and consider where your potential clients are most likely to view it.

Think Piece

Thought Leadership and the Competitive Advantage

By Cheryl Bame*

In today's hyper-connected and competitive professional landscape, establishing yourself as a thought leader isn't just a nice-to-have—it's become essential for female attorneys who are working to establish or advance their careers. Yet for busy female professionals juggling demanding schedules, the prospect of developing thought leadership can feel overwhelming. Success lies in understanding that authentic thought leadership isn't about becoming the loudest voice in the room, but about being the most insightful one.

The Strategic Imperative of Thought Leadership

When executed effectively, content could influence how others perceive your professional value and open doors that traditional networking cannot. Professionals who embrace this effort don't just advance their careers—they influence conversations.

We have heard from numerous in-house counsel panels that they value attorneys who can synthesize complex information, offer unique perspectives and effectively communicate ideas. This just isn't about self-promotion; it's about becoming a trusted source of insights that others value.

---

* Cheryl Bame is Principal of Bame Public Relations. A communications professional with enviable contacts and reach, Cheryl is widely recognized for her counsel and services to law firms and lawyers around the United States. After a decade in the broadcast news business, Cheryl has spent close to twenty-four years implementing communications programs that involve media relations, social media, thought leadership, networking, speaking engagements and other professional reputations strategies.

The Content-Driven Personal Brand Advantage

Building a personal brand through intelligent content offers several compelling advantages for busy professionals:

Scalable Influence: Unlike one-on-one networking, thoughtful content reaches hundreds or thousands of people simultaneously, especially if you know how to amplify it. A single well-crafted article or media quote can generate connections and opportunities that would take months to achieve through traditional relationship-building. It also makes it easier to boost your professional bio and your LinkedIn profile. It provides you with the opportunity to create client alerts and contribute to industry publications.

Credibility Amplification: When you share valuable insights, you're not just telling people you're an expert—you're demonstrating it. This proof-of-expertise approach builds trust more effectively than any resume or credentials list.

Opportunity Magnetism: Quality content acts as a beacon for opportunities. Speaking engagements, media interviews and new business opportunities naturally gravitate toward those who have established themselves as thoughtful contributors to important conversations. Plus, it makes you easily found when potential clients are searching for experts on a topic.

The Intelligence Factor in Content Creation

What separates thoughtful content is the depth of insight and quality of thinking demonstrated. Intelligent content is not just summarizing a topic or court decision but helping your target audience understand the impacts it would have on an industry or a business. Plus, AI rewards this type of content by referencing it in Google searches or AI platform requests.

Synthesis Over Summarization: Rather than simply report what's happening in your industry, synthesize information from multiple sources to reveal patterns, implications, and opportunities that others might miss.

Forward-Looking Perspective: While others focus on a basic overview, thought leaders identify emerging trends and their potential impact. This predictive element positions you as someone who helps others prepare for what's coming, not just understand what's happening.

Practical Application: The best thought leadership content bridges the gap between high-level concepts and practical implementation. Your audience should walk away with both understanding of the issue and actionable insights.

Contrarian Courage: Don't be afraid to challenge conventional wisdom when your experience and analysis suggest a different perspective. When possible, respectful disagreement with established thinking often generates the most engaging and valuable discussions. This is especially true for opinion pieces.

The AI Search Revolution

The rise of AI-powered search tools like ChatGPT, Claude, and search engines with AI integration like Google have fundamentally changed how information is discovered and consumed. This shift creates opportunities for thought leaders who understand how to create content that AI systems value and reference.

AI search tools don't just index content—they evaluate quality, authority, and relevance when generating responses. When professionals consistently produce thoughtful, well-researched content, they increase their likelihood of being cited by AI systems across countless queries related to their expertise area. This creates a multiplier effect where a single piece of intelligent content can influence thousands of AI-generated responses over time.

The professionals who recognize this shift early and adapt their content strategy accordingly will find themselves with a significant competitive advantage.

Implementation Strategy for Time-Constrained Professionals

The key to sustainable thought leadership lies in efficiency and focus by concentrating on topics where you already possess deep knowledge and experience. This reduces research time and ensures authenticity in your content. Plus, thoughtful commentary on industry news, trends, or other people's insights can be equally valuable and requires less time investment, and many publications prefer shorter pieces that don't exceed 900 words.

To be even more efficient, you could transform presentations into articles, insights from news articles into social media posts and non-privileged client conversations into industry observations. Your existing professional activities contain content gold mines of ideas.

The Long-Term Perspective

The professionals who achieve lasting influence understand that thought leadership is not a sprint but a marathon. The compound effect of consistently sharing valuable insights creates momentum that becomes increasingly powerful over time.

The question isn't whether you have time to develop thought leadership—it's whether you can afford not to. In an increasingly competitive professional landscape, those who can articulate valuable insights and build trusted personal brands will find themselves with a competitive advantage.

Chapter 4

Mastering LinkedIn: A Wonderful Networking and Thought Leadership Tool

"For most of history, Anonymous was a woman."

—Virginia Woolf

LinkedIn has changed the paradigm for how lawyers can market. In many ways, it has given anyone who wants it a channel to disseminate thought leadership or news of their own accomplishments and to connect with an audience of their own selection. Think of LinkedIn as running your own broadcast network.

LinkedIn is extremely popular among lawyers and business professionals worldwide, particularly in the United States and Europe. The platform has more than 1.1 billion members, and while the United States is the country with the most users, more than 70% of the users are outside the country.

It's a great way to stay top of mind with clients, prospects and intermediaries, taking up less time and effort than it might if you were to consistently run a campaign of sending out client memos or a detailed newsletter. It also provides a low-key way to reach out to people. LinkedIn has been a game changer, particularly for smaller firms and individual lawyers. It allows them a reach and an ability to market that gives them the power to punch above their weight.

LinkedIn Activities

LinkedIn activity can be represented as a pie with three slices. The first slice is your profile page. This page should reflect your business and what you are best known for doing. It should provide insights into your approach to your work.

The second slice is outreach. This means using LinkedIn to connect with people. It goes beyond the idea of just accepting invitations and aims to have you connect and engage with prospects and influential people in your industry who you want to know.

The third slice is the content you generate. Content can be your comments on other people's posts, original content you write for LinkedIn, such as updates or articles, or materials you forward with commentary.

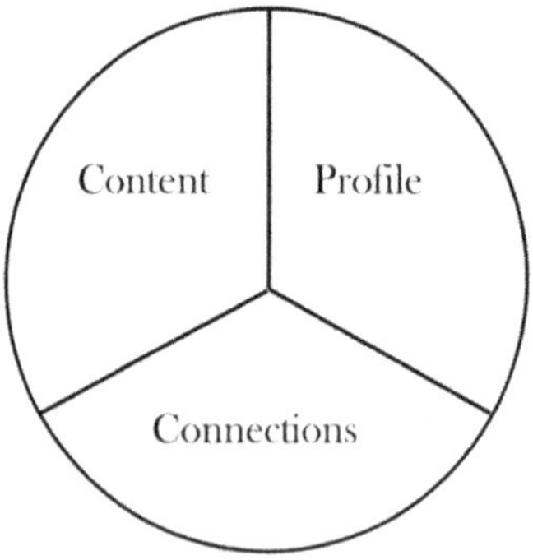

Your Profile

One of the first results that will come up when a potential client places your name in an online search will likely be your profile page on LinkedIn. With estimates of more than 90% of U.S. lawyers on the platform, it's vital to have a good profile.

A good professional photograph is a must, and it should be a photo that shows you with a business-like presence. I often tell clients to think of it as a representation of who a prospect will meet in person. A description of your title should include something about what you do. It should not simply read Partner at XYZ law firm, but rather "Commercial real estate partner focusing on biotech and manufacturing industries."

A banner photo, the rectangle behind your portrait shot, can be a corporate logo or a photo representing what you do for a living. An environmental lawyer I've worked with has a photo of the scales of justice covered with greenery. A New York litigator with whom I am friends has a modern skyscraper as his banner. There are graphic programs, such as Canva, and photo websites like Shutterstock, where you can subscribe to get the best quality photo for your banner. If you use other sources for photographs, make sure that the photo you use for your banner is royalty-free or arrange to comply with the photography platform you are using.

The About section of your LinkedIn profile should be written in the first person and say why you do what you do. It should also let your personality shine through. It is essential to get the About section right. Pay extra attention to the first few sentences. People have short attention spans and may not read much beyond that. Break up your paragraphs into short sentences, making them easier to read online. If you want to include deals or cases in this section, consider using bulleted lists to make it easier to digest the information.

The About section is an excellent place to include why you decided to pursue your area of law or to explain why you enjoy practicing in a particular industry. Aim to include search terms that people may use when looking for a lawyer within the field.

You can use up to 2600 characters. If you include a lot of text, you can make it even easier for a page visitor to read by using short paragraphs and incorporating white space between them.

In addition, the Feature section is important as it's a great way to customize and highlight those items you are most proud of that reflect how you want to be known. This section allows you to take the items, such as those you've posted in the past, and make them prominent in a fixed position when anyone visits your profile.

You may also want to place new material in the Featured section. For example, a featured item might be a link to the firm's website, an article you've written or a video you've created. You can add as many featured items as you want, add or remove content anytime, and easily change the order of the items.

Your Connections

It's great to connect with others on LinkedIn. Think about your contacts from today and from the past. Research shows that if someone once thought highly of you—even if they have not seen you in twenty years—if they remember you, they will generally think well of you today.

I admit that until my third year on LinkedIn, I didn't go out of my way to make new connections on the platform. Once I did, I learned that including a brief note along with my invitation, where LinkedIn allowed it, made it much more likely that I could establish a connection and add that person to my network. It also made it more likely that an online conversation with the contact would develop.

Some sources to consider when building your network:

- People with whom you currently work
- People with whom you have worked with in the past
- Classmates from law school and college

- People you grew up with from your hometown
- Association presidents and board members of those groups you want to pursue
- People who serve on committees or boards with you, even outside of work
- Leaders of the industry in which you are active
- Journalists who cover the topics in which you have an interest

Having a diverse group of connections is important. It's often a good indicator of success. It can lead to greater and more interesting collaboration and greater exposure to new people. It also allows you to be open to new opportunities. LinkedIn is a great way to start putting this premise into action.

When inviting people to connect, always take advantage of the LinkedIn pop-up that asks if you would like to write a note to the person with whom you are seeking to connect. As noted above from my own experience, writing a note that goes along with a request to connect provides a meaningful touchpoint and makes it more likely that your request to connect will be accepted.

Develop a habit of sending new people you meet a request to connect on LinkedIn. It's a great way of keeping your network up to date. Another idea: Consider creating a monthly reminder in your calendar to add new people to your LinkedIn network.

For more on networks, see https://www.robcross.org, the website of Professor Rob Cross, Edward A. Madden Professor of Global Leadership at Babson College, who has written and spoken extensively on this topic.

Your Content

When thinking about your niche, consider two or three subject areas for which you want to be known. They could be real estate and tax or securities litigation and volunteering for civil rights initiatives. Generally, a practice or an industry is a good first choice, but so is something more personal, such as a cause that matters to you. Once you have those areas mapped out, you can consider creating content that applies to one or more.

Content can be a short article, a comment on someone else's piece, or a link to an interesting article with a comment explaining why it's of interest. On LinkedIn, thought leadership posts get three times as many shares as other posts.[1]

Create and post content regularly to build your audience. Posting one article every three weeks is a good start.

Posts that include personal viewpoints or provide unique insight into an issue get more attention from viewers and receive higher circulation by LinkedIn's algorithm. Posts that forward content without commentary or give just a thumbs-up "like" symbol on someone else's post don't receive wide circulation.

Include links to the people you've named or the associations you may have referenced in your post. When you link to them, they will be notified that you have recognized them in your post and will likely help the post reach more people. By linking to them, not only will the individual be more likely to comment on the post, but the algorithm will share it with people who follow the individuals you've mentioned in the post. You can find those organizations' and individuals' links by using the @ sign and viewing the options. It may take some advanced planning before posting, but including the proper @ sign can exponentially extend your reach.

The right graphic attached to a post can have a big impact on viewership. Using an image that you create yourself—whether by personally taking a photograph or generating an image using artificial intelligence or in some other way—generally results in more views for the post than if you were to use no graphic or stock photography.

---

1. *See* Dilawar Malik, *100 Essential LinkedIn Statistics and Facts for 2025: Your Guide to the Professional Network*, LinkedIn (Mar. 11, 2025), https://www.linkedin.com/pulse/100-essential-linkedin-statistics-facts-2025-your-guide-dilawar-malik-pog9f/.

Personal human-interest stories have become more popular since the pandemic; however, if a post is more personal, it should still tie back to a business theme.

Once you've posted an item, respond to any comments within the first few hours of your posting. The LinkedIn algorithm views those stories as more active and successful and will share them more widely with a larger audience.

Draft your post before entering it online. LinkedIn allows users to edit their posts once they are published and live; however, if edits are made after a post is live and too much time elapses, LinkedIn reduces the number of viewers to whom the post is circulated. Aim to draft your post along with hashtags and @ links before posting it on LinkedIn to avoid the chance that you'll need revisions.

Success Stories and Real-World Examples

For Julie Spinelli, a partner at Le 16 Law, LinkedIn is a tool of both freedom and, a reflection of everything she does, great precision. As a lawyer in Paris, she utilizes the platform to connect with her clients around the world. She shares conference updates, contributes thought leadership, and posts about her recent publications. What stands out in her approach is not rigid scheduling or performative polish but a thoughtful and consistent effort to authentically showcase her work. "We are so lucky to have LinkedIn. It's a free marketing tool," Julie says. "I can see other lawyers posting things I love, even if I might not do it the same way. Everyone can bring their angle."

> "At the beginning of the year, I told myself I would post every fifteen days. Sometimes I miss it, but I just get back on the horse. It's like going to the gym. Just because you missed it doesn't mean you stop."
>
> **—Julie Spinelli**

Julie admits that keeping up a regular cadence can be time-consuming, especially during busy periods when she's in the midst of an arbitration, but she's developed a forgiving mindset about it. "At the beginning of the year, I told myself I would post every fifteen days. Sometimes, I miss it, but I just get back on the horse. It's like going to the gym. Just because you missed it doesn't mean you stop."

For women who hesitate to share content or fear they must be perfect, Julie's approach is a permission slip: Start small, be yourself, and know that consistency comes in many forms.

Nicole Cocozza, a business litigation lawyer at Prince Lobel Tye in Boston, has built a strong professional presence by demonstrating authenticity. She is highly intentional about community engagement. Early in her career, Nicole took a partner's advice to heart and began attending events hosted by the Massachusetts Bar Association's Young Lawyers Division. She gradually took on more responsibility—first as an attendee, then as a panelist, and eventually as division chair. Along the way, Nicole also connected with law students, professional associations, and even accountants to grow a well-rounded network. Her approach is consistent: Invest early, stay visible, and build authentic relationships. "It's not about getting business right away," she says, "but about building a solid reputation so that when people need someone they can trust, they think of you."

"It's not about getting business right away but about building a solid reputation so that when people need someone they can trust, they think of you."

—Nicole Cocozza

Nicole made LinkedIn an active part of her outreach strategy. She uses it to celebrate achievements, gain insights for her professional life, and promote causes she cares about—like running marathons for women's charities. By illustrating her work and values, she's stays top-of-mind with former colleagues and classmates, some of whom have sent her referrals. One recent example is her LinkedIn connection to a fellow American Bar Association member, who helped her identify the right lawyer in Nevada for a case her firm handled. She says, "LinkedIn helped me connect the dots—and it reminded others what I do and where I'm based in terms of my firm." For Nicole, LinkedIn isn't just a broadcast tool; it's a business development platform rooted in generosity and trust.

Gayle Klein is a nationally recognized commercial litigator known for her high-profile victories in a range of complex financial disputes and for defending against class actions.

As the co-head of U.S. litigation, arbitration and global investigations at Freshfields, Gayle's work as a lawyer is as clear-eyed as her approach to social media. She is thoughtful about the permanence and power of posting content. Her rule: Never post anything you wouldn't want your mother—or a client—to see. Gayle encourages younger lawyers to use platforms like LinkedIn to celebrate professional wins and build visibility, but always with intention. She believes that it's essential to balance both value and authenticity. She referenced a viral moment from a colleague who wore a T-shirt that read, "I'm the lawyer my mother wanted me to marry," as a smart, memorable example of how personality and message can intersect powerfully.

Strategies for Writing Posts That Will Make an Impact

Roy Sexton is the former President of the Legal Marketing Association and the Chief Marketing Officer at Vedder Price. Known for his sharp insights, wit, and deep commitment to inclusion, Roy has become a widely respected voice on personal branding, leadership authenticity, and legal marketing dynamics.

> "I can engage with people on a scale, in my time, asynchronously, and help create a footprint for who I am, what I like, what I enjoy."
>
> **—Roy Sexton**

Roy offers a refreshingly honest take on why social media can be a powerful—and underutilized—tool for professionals, especially those who don't naturally thrive in traditional networking environments. "I'm an introvert," he explains. "I don't go into a bar and make a thousand friends." He recalls hiding in the bathroom during a mortgage industry event, sipping a gin and tonic until he dared to go out and mingle. That discomfort led him to embrace social media as a means to connect with others authentically—and on his own terms. "I can engage with people on a scale, in my time, asynchronously, and help create a footprint for who I am, what I like, what I enjoy."

For Roy, social media isn't about chasing likes or obsessing over engagement metrics. It's about being consistently visible and helpful. "Some people think, 'Well, that post didn't get all the reaction.' I don't care," he says. "My mother used to say, 'The soup will speak for itself.'" Instead of striving for perfection, Roy encourages lawyers to jot down simple, valuable insights—the kinds of questions clients ask repeatedly—and share them in plain English. "It doesn't have to be six paragraphs. Give me a couple of sentences, and just do it."

He also emphasizes authenticity in both what he posts and the advice he offers to lawyers. "If you're a theater person, talk about that. If you support the LGBTQ community, share that. Show the flavors of who you are." The result? When someone meets Roy in person, they already feel like they know him—and he believes that authenticity builds real trust.

Quick Tips for Getting Started

- Define your goals and target audience.
- Optimize your LinkedIn profile (particularly your photo, headline and About section).
- Create a simple content plan (topics to cover, frequency of posting, hashtags).
- Start connecting with meaningful people from your past and present.
- Share and repurpose bylined articles.
- Post at least once every three weeks and reply to comments.
- Remember, be authentic, not perfect.

Think Piece

The 6 Ps of LinkedIn Impact for Women Lawyers

By Nancy Myrland*

I know that sometimes LinkedIn can feel like a minefield. You're told to "put yourself out there," but you've also been taught not to be too visible, too loud, or too self-promotional.

That tension is real, especially for women lawyers navigating professional expectations, firm culture, and internal and external pressure to "do it right." But here's what I've learned from years of helping lawyers use LinkedIn: the platform doesn't reward perfection. It rewards clarity, consistency, and connection. When women show up as they really are—smart, thoughtful, and client-focused—it works.

To help guide that process, I teach what I call *The 6 Ps of LinkedIn*. It's a practical framework for women lawyers (and any professional) who want to use LinkedIn to build their reputation and relationships, amplify expertise, and stay top of mind.

1. Permission

Before anything else, you need permission, your own.

I want you to believe you're worthy of being seen and heard. You need to know it's okay to use this space to share your knowledge,

* Nancy Myrland, President of Myrland Marketing & Social Media, is a legal marketing and business development advisor specializing in content, LinkedIn strategy, podcasting, video, and AI consulting for lawyers and legal professionals. A LinkedIn Top Voice and member of the LMA Hall of Fame, she helps lawyers elevate their presence, expand their reach, and connect with clients in ways that build trust and drive results. She can be contacted directly at nancy@myrlandmarketing.com or through her website, https://www.myrlandmarketing.com/.

your perspective, and your personality. All of those belong on LinkedIn and in every space you occupy.

This is the "P" I didn't include in my original model, but I've come to realize it's foundational. Without permission, the remaining Ps don't matter.

2. Planning

LinkedIn isn't just about posting. It's about purpose. What do you want to be known for? Who are you trying to reach? Once you know that, your strategy becomes simpler and more sustainable. Planning also cuts down on the time you spend wondering what to post.

3. Profile

Your profile is your 24/7 ambassador. It should reflect your practice, your personality, and your point of view.

- Writing your About section in a voice that sounds like you
- Using your headline to highlight more than your title
- Adding media, certifications, and projects that show the depth of your work

Yes, a great photo matters. Show up the way you want to be remembered.

4. Presence

This is where the magic happens. Presence means showing up, not just with posts, but with engagement. Comment. Congratulate. Ask thoughtful questions.

You don't have to *create* every day, but you can *connect* every day.

Take one of my favorite clients, a brilliant healthcare lawyer in the United States. We've been working on launching her podcast, but LinkedIn has been part of the process all along.

Recently, she told me, "I've been hearing from people all over the healthcare industry, some I haven't seen in a while, that they're seeing me everywhere on LinkedIn. Not just my posts, but my interactions. They mean that in a good way."

She credits that shift to what we discuss about profile and presence.

5. Persistence

LinkedIn isn't "one and done." You don't post once and expect business to roll in.

You show up consistently. You test. You learn what resonates. You stay visible, even when you're busy.

The lawyers who see results don't disappear when their calendars fill up. They understand that visibility is a form of credibility, and it compounds.

6. Patience

LinkedIn rewards those who play the long game. It's not always instant, but over time, your presence builds trust. The person who reads your post today may recommend you months from now. The GC who sees your comment may quietly follow you before ever reaching out.

This isn't performance. It's positioning, and it works.

Bonus: Video Builds Trust Quickly

Want to build trust faster? Use video.

No need for a studio. A simple one-minute clip, even taken on your phone, can go a long way.

Feeling adventurous? Try LinkedIn Live. Host a ten-minute conversation with a colleague or client. Let people hear your voice, see your face, and connect with how you think.

Women lawyers are often natural communicators. Video just magnifies and accelerates that strength.

What Law Firms Can Do to Help

Law firms don't need to control LinkedIn. But they do need to support it.

- Encourage lawyers to build out their profiles
- Recognize LinkedIn visibility as legitimate business development
- Share and amplify lawyers' content
- Provide guidance, not just restrictions

LinkedIn is not optional. In other industries, it is a business development necessity. Legal should not lag behind.

Closing Thought

LinkedIn is not a stage. It is a table, a place where your clients, colleagues, and future connections are already gathered.

Effective use means showing up, speaking honestly and genuinely, and trusting that your voice belongs.

The 6 Ps—Permission, Planning, Profile, Presence, Persistence, and Patience—can guide the way. And the results? They are more than visible. They are lasting.

Chapter 5

Getting the Most Benefit from Speaking Engagements

"Women speaking up for themselves and for those around them is the strongest force we have to change the world."

—Melinda Gates

Some people hesitate to take on speaking engagements because they are anxious about speaking in public or serving on panels. They are not alone. Up to 75% of the population has a fear of public speaking.[1]

Often, I hear from men and women that they don't want to make a presentation because they won't have anything valuable to add, or they are fearful about making mistakes in front of an audience. Others worry about the time commitment involved in

---

1. *See* Alexandre Heeren et al., *Assessing public speaking fear with the short form of the Personal Report of Confidence as a Speaker scale: confirmatory factor analyses among a French-speaking community sample*, Neuropsychiatric Disease Treatment, volume 2013:9 at 609 (May 3, 2013), https://pmc.ncbi.nlm.nih.gov/articles/PMC3647380/.

preparation and delivery, or feel unsure about how to turn a speaking engagement into an actual business opportunity. And for those who are already busy, the idea of adding yet another responsibility to their calendar can seem overwhelming. I know that feeling.

Preparing for a Speaking Engagement and Calming Your Nerves

If you are anxious about public speaking, the following steps will give you confidence that can help offset your nerves.

1. ***Know your topic inside out.*** The more familiar you are with the subject matter, the less likely you'll lose your place. Anticipate potential audience questions and prepare clear answers. Confidence in your content is a powerful antidote to nerves. Also, remember, you are asked to speak to the particular audience because presumably, you'll know more than they do, and they want to hear from you. The audience is there to learn from you, not to judge you.
2. ***Get organized early.*** Prepare your presentation, including any slides or props, and practice using them. Don't go overboard with PowerPoints. Practice to make sure you'll get through all of the slides without rushing at the end. Visit the venue in advance, test the equipment, and rehearse there if possible. If that's not possible, ask the organizers to send you a photo of the room so that you can get an idea of the layout. Such preparation is one way to reduce some of your anticipatory anxiety.
3. ***Practice, practice, practice.*** Rehearse your talk multiple times—alone, in front of trusted friends, and even in front of a camera. Cell phones are perfect for this. Even if I know a presentation cold, I usually spend time practicing in front of a camera or recording myself on Zoom (just

for me to see). Watch yourself, give yourself feedback, and refine your delivery. The more you practice, the more natural and confident you'll feel.

4. ***Visualize success.*** Picture yourself delivering a clear, engaging talk. Imagine the audience nodding and responding positively. A positive mental rehearsal can shift your mindset from anxiety to optimism.
5. ***Ground yourself physically.*** Relax your shoulders, take deep breaths, and use natural gestures to feel more composed. The type of power posing that social psychologist Amy Cuddy, author of *Presence: Bringing Your Boldest Self to Your Biggest Challenges*, made popular, can also be a big help in this area.
6. ***Practice using pauses.*** If you momentarily lose your place, simply pause, breathe, and pick up where you left off. Pauses often feel longer to the speaker than they do to the audience. When rehearsing, use pauses to think about where to take natural breaks.
7. ***Seek support if needed.*** Consider joining a group like Toastmasters or working with a coach or mentor. They can provide feedback, practice opportunities, and a sense of community.
8. ***Celebrate Every Speaking Experience.*** After your talk, acknowledge what went well, even small wins. Reflect on what you can improve on next time and recognize that mistakes are natural and part of the growth process.

The Power of Reputation

One benefit of speaking on a panel, besides the opportunity to share what you know, is to have a field of interest or a niche affiliated with your profile.

"Don't just network—build a reputation."

—Heather Nevitt

"Don't just network—build a reputation," advises Heather Nevitt, Editor-in-Chief of *Corporate Counsel* at ALM. In her view, it's not about how many people know your name, but what they associate with your name. The most successful lawyers aren't those who chase every opportunity—they're those known for something specific. "You want people to think of you when a particular kind of problem arises," she says. "That's when your name becomes a solution, not just a contact."

Heather emphasizes intentionality over volume. "You don't have to be on every panel every week. But if you're thoughtful and consistent, people start associating you with quality, expertise, and trust. Your reputation becomes an asset in motion—something that grows stronger over time and outlasts any single deal."

Content That Resonates

Professional speakers, those whose primary income is derived from speaking engagements, know that it's important to be yourself. Use humor, tell a story, and connect with the audience as a real person. Authenticity builds rapport and reduces pressure.

At Lowenstein Sandler LLP, Lynda Bennett is chair of the firm's Insurance Recovery Group, co-founder of the firm's Women's Initiative Network, which she has led for the past decade, and a longstanding member on the firm's Executive Board and Compensation Committee. Through her practice, she has secured billions of dollars in insurance recoveries for her clients. Lesley Adamo, vice chair of Lowenstein's Tax Group, is a member of the firm's Executive Board, Inclusion Committee, and Strategic Planning leadership team. Both women emphasize the importance of being thoughtful, strategic, and authentic when it comes to public-facing content, whether that be in the form of a panel, a keynote speech, and presence on social media.

"The posts and other media communications that get the biggest response aren't about me—they're about something bigger than myself. That's what resonates."

—Lynda Bennett

Lynda, who also appears on podcasts and panels, says the most meaningful content isn't self-promotional—it's personal. "The posts and other media communications that get the biggest response aren't about me—they're about something bigger than myself. That's what resonates." She also believes in keeping it short, useful, and—when possible—a little funny. Lynda is more than a little funny. She describes her practice as "suing insurance companies with a smile on my face," making it more likely with that catch phrase she'll be remembered for her substance when she speaks on a panel or a podcast.

Lesley echoes the value of substance over style: "I was once invited to join an M&A podcast, and afterwards, a number of listeners reached out to ask me for tax advice in structuring their transactions as a result of what was discussed during the program. That's when I knew it landed." For both women, content is about building trust and delivering value, not noise. "There's already too much content out there," Lynda said. "I tell others be clear, be helpful, and speak like a human."

Charlyn Ho is a former Cravath associate and Perkins Coie partner who had a successful career in the Navy and Big Law before starting her own law firm, Rikka, a boutique firm focusing on intellectual property, technology and privacy. Charlyn has a coach who encouraged her to do more to market her firm and to become more visible and less reserved online. One piece of advice from her coach was simple but powerful: When at a conference—whether speaking or just as an attendee—she should take photos and post them with a short update, signaling her presence and involvement.

Initially hesitant, Charlyn began experimenting with this approach. At first, she wasn't sure anyone would be interested. However, the results were surprising. At an AI conference Charlyn attended, she took a picture of herself with her conference badge and posted the photograph to her social media. The post garnered more than 100 likes—far more engagement than she anticipated. The experience highlighted something important: Charlyn's growing presence at conferences reflects not only her expertise, but also her willingness to show up, share, and connect.

Strategic Speaking Engagements

Make sure that your speaking engagements—like any other business development activity—align with your niche, strengths and audience's interests.

You can end up wasting a lot of time on speaking engagements if you're not careful. If you say yes to groups that don't align with your practice, or topics far from your expertise, you risk diluting your efforts. You miss the chance to connect with the right audience. It's important to be selective and strategic—otherwise, you're just spinning your wheels.

If your speaking choices are wise, these engagements offer a powerful way to cement your expertise and build strong visibility. When you create speaker content, it can always be amplified and used in other formats. A speech transcript can be turned into webinar content or a bylined article. The key is preparation and connection, as well as maximizing the opportunity beyond the moment.

Mary Wilson is a Partner at Dentons US and a member of its Regional and Global Boards. Having completed five years as the Dentons US Managing Partner, she currently serves as Global Vice-Chair for the US Region. She is refreshingly frank about what works for her and what doesn't. She doesn't use social media and isn't active on LinkedIn. Yet she pushed herself to get comfortable with public speaking early in her career—not to build visibility, but to improve her communication skills and deepen her subject-matter expertise. "When you present something publicly, you dig in deeper," she said. She also stressed that lawyers should not feel they need to do everything. "If you hate some sort of marketing, you can try it occasionally, but it shouldn't be the core of your business development plan."

The right type of speaking engagement will land you in front of a crowd of potential clients or referral sources, and if you're lucky or have a choice in the matter, your panelists will also be people in a position to send business to you. In addition, this is a great way to meet other panelists who may be giving lots of talks. If they are impressed with your performance, they may ask you to join them on other panels or association projects.

The best approach to speaking engagements is to ground your activity in preparation and connection. Most lawyers will want to prepare because they are intent on delivering value. The best speeches give people in the audience a positive feeling and help them remember a few important messages. But besides ensuring that you are knowledgeable on the topic, preparation helps calm your nerves and, in the case of working on panels, time spent with co-panelists preparing together often can lead to growing new contacts.

Lynda at Lowenstein always insists on a prep call with fellow panelists. "Chemistry matters. I want to know who I'm sitting with, how we complement each other, and how we make the session engaging together. You're not just delivering content; you're creating an experience."

> "Let people know you're speaking. Engage with the audience beforehand—make the room warm before you even walk in."
>
> **—Lesley Adamo**

She and Lesley also emphasize pre- and post-event strategy. Lynda says, "Let people know you're speaking. Engage with the audience beforehand—make the room warm before you even walk in." And afterward? "Follow up. Say thank you. Turn the talk into a blog or a post. That's your intellectual property. Use it again. Don't let it live and die in one room." Her approach turns every speaking engagement into a multi-touch opportunity to grow visibility and build trust.

Nadège Nguyen is a partner in the Paris office of Gide Loyrette Nouel, a highly regarded international law firm based in France. A member of the Corporate Mergers & Acquisitions team, Nadège has spent her career building a strong international reputation through a combination of legal excellence and deeply personal relationships. A former Chair of the Lex Mundi association of law firms, Nadège knows the value of patience, consistency, and finding ways over the long run to make business development feel natural and authentic through a network of clients, referral sources and friends.

She's quick to note that business development takes time. "The feedback only comes after years and years of involvement," she says. Nadège has developed several strategies, including speaking engagements, for making herself visible in the legal and business communities without ever coming across as self-promotional.

"I always suggest the names of a few friends to join me on a panel, such as general counsel or peers. I may not have any business from them, but I want to showcase their career and their expertise," she explains. "I do this by getting them involved in a program, and they like it. It helps them develop their own profile. And maybe one day, you never know."

> "I believe in building links without pressure."
>
> **—Nadège Nguyen**

This approach reflects her long-game mindset: If she can elevate others and create meaningful moments of connection, opportunities will follow. It's a strategy based not just on networking, but on generosity. "I believe in building links without pressure," she says. "It's not always about asking for an assignment."

Maximizing Your Marketing Efforts

If you've spoken at a great industry conference, especially in a sector you're hoping to break into, but you don't let anyone know, you've limited the potential payoff. You may have learned a lot and made some fantastic connections, but that's just the beginning. To maximize the value of attending, you need to amplify what you've gained from the experience and showcase your involvement.

Speaking engagements are not just a matter of showing up and giving a talk. The actual speech should be considered just one step in the middle of a marketing process. You can make the most of your efforts by doing some advance due diligence, and after the talk, some post-program work.

Here are some activities to help you market, before and after a presentation.

In advance

- Write a LinkedIn post highlighting a key insight from your upcoming talk and tag the conference and other speakers.
- Ask for a list of potential attendees. By reviewing it, you can further focus your talk, and also if appropriate, plan advanced reach-outs to people you expect to see.
- Preview your topic and share what you're most excited about in order to build anticipation.
- Email relevant clients and contacts, letting them know about your talk and offering to discuss the topic in more detail.
- Research and connect with fellow speakers or attendees in advance to warm up your network.

After the Event

- Post a short video on social media sharing your favorite takeaway or a behind-the-scenes glimpse from the conference.
- Request a video clip of your talk from the organizers to share on your website or LinkedIn.
- Write a client alert, blog post, or article summarizing your talk, linking back to the event.
- Add the talk to your bio and firm website under speaking engagements with a brief description.
- Include your talk in your firm's next newsletter to reinforce your expertise.

- If you can get a list of people who attended, you can send them follow-up notes.
- Follow up with new contacts you met at the event with a personalized note or LinkedIn connection request.
- Offer to send attendees a resource mentioned during your talk (e.g., a red flags checklist or a summary of your key points) in order to gather contact information and cultivate leads.
- Keep a running list of events you've spoken at for future pitches, bios, and internal tracking.
- Repurpose the content in multiple ways—use snippets for social media posts, include highlights in presentations, or reference insights in future client conversations.

The follow-up that comes after an event is of great value.

Taking the Extra Steps

David Ackert, CEO of PipelinePlus and author of *The Short List: How to Drive Business Development by Focusing on the People Who Matter Most*, says, "When it comes to speaking engagements, most people forget to ask themselves, 'What outcome am I actually aiming for?' It's not just about giving the talk—it's about what happens next. Too often, people assume a presentation is simply a way to grow their brand, but a more meaningful goal is to spark one-on-one conversations with prospective clients in the audience. Structure your presentation with that specific outcome in mind."

David is a master at turning passive listeners into active participants. "I might prepare ten key points but only share six, leaving room to adapt to the audience and engage in the moment. I pepper in questions that invite conversation—sometimes I'll even say, 'Write your questions down and pass them up. I'll answer as many as I can.' These moments bring the room to life and create natural opportunities for personal follow-ups afterward."

One great technique is to mention a resource during your talk that you can send out afterwards to interested members of the audience. For example, if you were to give a talk on the Foreign Corrupt Practices Act, you might mention that you have a list of red flags for FCPA vulnerabilities. You can offer to share the document and ask people to leave you their business card or otherwise send you their name and contact information. By doing this, you'll cultivate leads with whom you can open a dialogue. And if you add them to your LinkedIn connections, you can remain in touch. Such contacts may even become potential clients.

Focusing on what you are going to say and the value you are bringing to your audience can go a long way toward overcoming obstacles and giving a great presentation. Only by speaking up and being out in front of the market we want to pursue can we let people know what type of work we want to take on.

Think Piece

The Power of Public Speaking: Feel the Fear and Do It Anyway

By Melissa Davis*

As Susan Jeffers said in her bestselling book, *Feel the Fear and Do It Anyway*, stepping outside your comfort zone is where the growth really happens. Nowhere is that more true than with public speaking. Whether it's a panel at a legal conference, a keynote at an industry event, or simply introducing yourself on a webinar, public speaking is one of the most powerful ways to build your personal brand.

Over the years, as I've built my own profile, both personally and through MD Communications, I've found that speaking opportunities often follow visibility. And then they keep coming. But while it may look from the outside like I enjoy public speaking (and often I do), that doesn't mean I don't hear the same voices many of you do.

"Why have they asked me?"

"What do I know about this?"

"Wow, look who else is on the panel . . ."

These are the imposter thoughts that have accompanied me to stages from London to New York to Tokyo. I've woken up at 3 a.m. wondering if I've said yes to something I can't deliver. But here's the truth: I've never regretted saying yes to the *right* opportunities.

---

* Melissa Davis is the founder of MD Communications, a leading legal PR and reputation management agency built on nearly two decades of experience, trusted relationships, and a values-driven approach to client service. A frequent IBA speaker and advocate for diversity, she co-founded the Positive Parenting Alliance and sits on several global legal advisory boards, championing inclusion, wellbeing, and impact in the legal sector.

In fact, public speaking has taken me to some incredible places including, memorably, training the President of the Maldives back in 2009. It's helped me grow my network, build credibility, and most importantly, build relationships that have turned into both work and long-term partnerships.

So how do you feel the fear and do it anyway?

Here are my top tips to keep that 3 a.m. anxiety monster at bay:

1. Make sure the opportunity is right for you.

Fear isn't always a sign to back away. Sometimes it's a sign you're stretching in exactly the right way. That said, don't say yes to something completely misaligned with your skills or audience. That's a recipe for panic, not growth.

Start with audiences you feel some connection to. If you've never done a panel before, don't start with a 500-person keynote. Stretch, don't snap.

2. Know your audience.

I'm a PR expert, so I'll always say this, but knowing your audience is everything. Are you speaking to partners, GCs, early-career lawyers, or business services professionals? What do they care about right now? What do they need from you?

For example, if I'm speaking to law firm marketing teams, I'll lead with practical tips they can use tomorrow. But if I'm speaking to managing partners, I'll tie my points into strategy, reputation, and long-term growth. Tailor the tone and message and you'll instantly feel more confident.

3. What's the headline?

Think back to the best talk you've ever been to. Do you remember every point? Probably not. But I bet you remember one powerful line or idea.

A great talk is like a great piece of PR—it's built around clear, memorable messaging. You need one to three key takeaways you want your audience to remember. If you can't sum up your talk in a single sentence, you're trying to say too much.

One of my most shared talks was titled: *"Don't Be Boring on LinkedIn."* That was the headline and the whole talk unpacked how to make your content stand out while being authentic.

4. Connect with the panel.

If you're on a panel, don't wait until you're backstage to say hello. Connect with fellow speakers on LinkedIn before the event, send a quick message, or join the prep call. You'll feel more at ease, you'll build genuine rapport, and you might just gain a new friend or collaborator.

5. Practice.

As golfer Gary Player said, "The more I practice, the luckier I get." The same goes for speaking. Rehearse your opening. Practice key messages out loud. Don't try to memorize the whole thing, but do give your talk some muscle memory.

No one is a "natural." Those speakers who seem effortless? They've just done the work.

6. Breathe, connect, smile.

This one sounds simple, but it matters. When you're nervous, your breath gets shallow. Take a few deep breaths before you start. Smile at the audience. Make eye contact. Open with a relatable question or a quick story to draw people in.

And if you forget a point, don't panic. You're not delivering a court judgment. You're there to tell a story, to inform and connect.

7. Treat it like a media interview.

Here's the part many lawyers forget: speaking gigs are like media interviews. You need to keep it simple, stick to your key messages, and avoid getting lost in too much technical detail. You're not showing how much you know, you're helping your audience understand what matters.

The same rules apply: don't try to say everything. Be clear. Be relevant and leave them wanting more.

8. Have a PR strategy.

Make your talk work harder. Post on LinkedIn before the event, tag the organizers, and let your network know you're speaking. Share your slides or a soundbite after. Use it as an opportunity to raise your profile and show your expertise.

And don't forget to follow up with people you meet at the event. Relationships start in the room, but they grow in the follow-up.

Final thought

Public speaking is a muscle and it gets stronger every time you use it. You don't have to love it. But if you want to grow your brand, raise your profile, and open doors, it's one of the most valuable skills you can develop.

And remember: you don't need to be perfect. You just need to be yourself, prepared, passionate, and clear . . . and lastly, try and enjoy it.

Chapter 6

Navigating Networks and Associations

"I am not afraid of storms, for I am learning how to sail my ship."

—Louisa May Alcott

Deborah Enix-Ross, now a senior advisor at Debevoise & Plimpton and a former American Bar Association (ABA) President, grew up in Harlem as the daughter of a mother who worked as a file clerk and a father who was a short-order cook. She was the first in her family to graduate high school, college and law school. Deborah always knew she wanted to be a lawyer, though she wasn't certain how to get there, given her background. But according to Deborah, "That 'first generation' determination gave me a special kind of strength."

Determined, she did attend law school, and soon after graduating, Deborah used her graduation gift money to attend her first ABA meeting—before she even knew her bar results. Alone in San Francisco, she walked into the International Law Section of the ABA and was welcomed by the lawyers. As Deborah recounts the story, "There weren't many women in the room. And there were even fewer people of color. But the people who were there—they welcomed me. They supported me. They saw something in me, and that gave me the courage to keep going."

Reflecting back, she says, "That was gutsy—but there's nothing like the confidence of youth."

Today, she encourages young lawyers to trust their instincts and know they belong.

Confidence, even without a written roadmap, can help open doors and build lasting connections.

Formal Networks and Associations

That first ABA meeting wasn't just the start of Deborah's career; it was the moment she found a place—a community—where she could grow. And it's been a rewarding journey for her ever since.

"If I could say one thing to young lawyers, it's this: Trust in the skills and instincts that got you to this point. Let that confidence carry you forward. You belong here."

—Deborah Enix-Ross

According to Deborah, "If I could say one thing to young lawyers, it's this: Trust in the skills and instincts that got you to this point. Let that confidence carry you forward. You belong here."

The ABA and International Bar Association (IBA) are two remarkable organizations that have been shaping the legal landscape for decades. The IBA was established in 1947, shortly after the creation of the United Nations, whereas the ABA dates to

1878. Yet, the world of legal associations has undergone significant evolution in recent years.

Groups like the Association of Corporate Counsel and various minority bar associations worldwide have emerged as indispensable—not just for visibility with clients, but also for fostering community, learning, and referrals. These aren't merely support networks; in many ways, they function as business accelerators. The insights gained from peers and the referrals that often flow from connections—whether a client needs representation in another state or country or a firm has a conflict but wants to recommend a trusted colleague—are invaluable for any lawyer looking to grow a robust book of business.

For many professionals, joining an association can be a transformative experience, although the benefits are often not immediately obvious.

Coach Carolyn Sandano reflected on her journey: "I don't think you understand all of the benefits of joining an association until you jump in and you're there. You start to realize the goals you have are shared by others. The worries, the self-doubt—they're shared too."

Over time, these shared experiences lead to something deeper. "You often find like minds and end up growing with them over decades," she said. "They become critical to your professional development, and in many cases, your personal development, too." Carolyn believes women, in particular, benefit from these affiliations: "Women affiliate more deeply and easily than men tend to. They look at the whole of a person and maintain those relationships longer."

Of course, entering a long-established group can be intimidating. "You have to come with an open mind," Carolyn advises. "Attend and be the new kid for a while and show up all the time. Volunteer. Make your involvement valuable to others. That's how you become part of the fabric." She emphasized the importance of small gestures—offering to host a meeting, manning the name tag table, or simply buying snacks. "It's about showing that you care," she said.

Getting involved in professional organizations has been a game-changer for Sara Koleilat-Aranjo, even though it happened by accident. "I didn't even know what the IBA was," she admitted. "One of my partners had an unexpected conflicts schedule and couldn't travel to Korea for the IBA Annual Conference, and asked if I could step in. That's how it started."

That one request led her to speaking engagements, leadership roles, and ultimately, her appointment as the first woman and youngest person to chair the Arab Regional Forum of the IBA. These experiences helped raise her profile globally and provided her with a platform to grow, both professionally and personally.

Informal Networks: Beyond the Associations

While formal networks offered by membership associations can be invaluable for developing a practice—especially if you engage with committees and take on roles that connect you with other members—it's equally important to recognize that lawyers already possess built-in networks. These personal and professional connections can be just as powerful, even outside the formal organizational structure.

Adam Severson is the Chief Marketing and Business Development Officer at Baker Donelson, a national law firm with more than 700 attorneys. Adam is also the Past President of the Legal Marketing Association. Adam knows the sales process within law firms like the back of his hand and has built a valuable network that would be the envy of any great rainmaker. He believes that for lawyers to build a network, they need to start with a simple step: first, look at who you know.

"We coach our lawyers to look at their network and see who's in there right now. I aim to get them to identify what I consider to be high-potential people—those individuals who just have 'it' and are going places. That could be an accountant, someone at a large consulting firm, or an entrepreneur who went to law school not necessarily to practice law, but because they saw it as a valuable credential to help secure funding for their idea."

Adam points out that understanding your own personal network is key.

He also believes that building a network means helping these lawyers to be inquisitive. "One of the biggest attributes of a successful networker, and eventually a rainmaker, is genuine curiosity—not just asking three questions from a sales checklist, but deeply and actively listening, engaging, and asking thoughtful follow-up questions."

Looking at legendary rainmakers, we can see that many women have created impressive networks on their own.

"You have to be organic to yourself. If you like writing, write. If you like speaking, speak. Let's figure out where you belong and build from there."

—Stacy Phillips

Stacy Phillips, one of the country's most respected family law attorneys, has developed her practice at Blank Rome not by following a script but by embracing what is authentic to her. Rather than conforming to the traditional business development playbook, which often involved golf outings, aggressive follow-up calls, or endless networking events, Stacy has built a career rooted in connection, generosity, and trust. She tells younger lawyers: "You have to be organic to yourself. If you like writing, write. If you like speaking, speak. Let's figure out where you belong and build from there." For Stacy, it's networking and an individual-centered approach that has allowed her to guide others in a way that feels both strategic and personal.

One of her signature moves is hosting dinner parties. Stacy has long used entertaining as a way to bring people together, especially when she sees an opportunity to help others make valuable connections. "If I can't help someone directly," she says, "I'll invite them to a dinner where they'll meet the right people."

These gatherings, which often include professionals from across industries, are not only memorable but meaningful—sparking referrals, business partnerships, and, on more than one occasion, even a romantic match. By creating a warm and collaborative environment, Stacy positions herself as a connector and trusted resource—without ever needing to make a hard ask.

For Stacy, business development is less about promoting oneself and more about showing up consistently and adding value. She's a believer in giving first. "The best way to get referrals from any network is to refer others," she says. She sends handwritten birthday cards, checks in with former clients and colleagues, and is intentional about maintaining relationships. Her approach is proof that authentic engagement, paired with a willingness to be generous to one's network, can be a powerful foundation for a thriving practice.

> "Don't fall into the trap of the Cinderella syndrome, expecting that if you just put your head down and do good work, people will notice and appreciate it. You have to get out there—and yes, sometimes you'll fall flat, but there will be many more times you will surprise yourself and others with measurable growth from those 'stretch' experiences."
>
> **—Lynda Bennett**

Lynda Bennett and Lesley Adamo, partners at Lowenstein Sandler LLP, believe that business development has become a blend of curiosity, consistency, authenticity, and purposeful action. "Stop committing random acts of lunch," Lynda advises with a smile. "Don't just go out for the sake of going out. Go with a purpose, know what you're hoping to learn, make sure you genuinely like your lunch date, and follow up." Lynda further advised, "Don't fall into the trap of the Cinderella syndrome, expecting that if you just put your head down and do good work, people will notice and appreciate it. You have to get out there—and yes, sometimes you'll fall flat, but there will be many more times you will surprise yourself and others with measurable growth from those 'stretch' experiences."

One of Lesley's biggest referral sources has become her network of accountants—not by design, but by collaborating on shared matters, doing good work, responding promptly, and being helpful. As a specialist, Lesley also views her corporate colleagues as clients. "I ask my corporate colleagues, 'How, as a tax lawyer, can I be most helpful to you and the client?' And then I have shaped how I communicate accordingly," she said. For Lynda, marketing began with writing articles and speaking on panels, even when she wasn't sure she belonged. "Honestly, I learned more about the 'big picture' concepts of my practice area by engaging in these kinds of activities early on in my career, which gave me double the return on my time investment: I was marketing and becoming a better lawyer at the same time. All of these lessons, looking at referrals, communicating your specific niche, and getting out are lessons she passes on to younger women lawyers.

Authentic Engagement and Making Networking Work for You

To build a network, as Adam Severson points out, you need to be inquisitive. Women may be particularly adept at this, as listening to people is the first step.

Catherine Zinn is Baker Botts' first-ever Chief Client Officer. She oversees various aspects of growth and strategy along with the firm's sector-focused client development, marketing and communications functions globally. She also highlighted listening as a powerful differentiator for women in business development. Catherine noted, "Clients don't operate in a vacuum; they work within organizations, each with its own complex dynamics." She says, "Women often listen on multiple levels—picking up on both the spoken and unspoken cues. They tend to ask more insightful questions and listen more attentively. I find that women are often better at listening and understanding the broader dynamics, which ultimately helps them serve as highly effective trusted advisors, advocates, and deal makers."

Catherine points out, "Doing service for charitable organizations or other causes creates a connection with fellow volunteers that is different than any other type of connection. As I reflect on some of the strongest relationships I have and how we formed such a close and meaningful connection, it was often by serving on a board together. When you work on hard and important issues together, you get to know each other well."

Authenticity and being strategic in how you network, entertain prospects, and remain in touch with clients is a must. The best social events are the ones in which both the lawyer and the client/prospect can have a shared interest.

Randi Revisore, Chief Business Development Officer at Vinson & Elkins and a former practicing lawyer, brings a practical and honest lens to the challenges and opportunities surrounding business development—especially for women in law. One of her central messages is that lawyers need to be deeply attuned to the lives and needs of their clients rather than relying on outdated or traditional business development tactics. "You meet them where they're at," she says. "That's not the traditional way of doing it."

She points out that if your client is a working parent, asking them to a 6:30 p.m. dinner might not be the most effective move. Instead, lawyers should consider alternatives—whether it's lunch, a weekend run, or attending a family-friendly event together. Randi says, "These adjustments are not about lowering expectations but about creating genuine, client-centered engagement that acknowledges real-world logistics."

When I spoke with Annalisa Reale at Chiomenti in Milan, she explained the approach she developed for business development.

"Growing up, I was a professional classical violinist. I was not a sports person. I was a music person. I played in string quartets, chamber groups, and symphonic orchestras. There is no better example of teamwork than being in an orchestra and performing a Wagner opera or the entire Ninth Symphony by Beethoven. You need to be a great performer, but then you need to be in a great orchestra."

Annalisa tried several ways of networking but understood that her best way to network was to bring people to great symphonic orchestra concerts or to La Scala, the famed opera house in Milan. "I will go to the opera myself, but I also love taking my clients and speaking about it afterwards over dinner."

"While it may be more difficult to network as a woman, as many of the lawyers in house are men, we can find our ways by looking at alternative networking, and this means alternative ways of business development based on sharing values and things you are truly passionate about and that defines what you are in professional and personal terms."

Annalisa points out that she is comfortable with her brand, because it is authentic to her.

Gide Loyrette Nouel partner Nadège Nguyen, makes time in Paris for personal hosting, also choosing environments that reflect her values and interests. "This year, I'm organizing female-only dinners at my home," she says. "I'll invite clients, prospects, partners, and counsel. Just small things. But it's up to you to create those moments of connection—and you can build them around things you enjoy."

One of her favorite events was an art-focused gathering she created at Gide, centered around female artists. "It was something that combined my personal interests with a meaningful opportunity to connect with others."

"It's a people business. You have to like people. You have to listen. And you have to show them that you care," she says. "If they feel that, the business will come—maybe not immediately, but eventually."

—Nadège Nguyen

For Nadège, visibility isn't about broadcasting one's accomplishments—it's about curating moments that matter. She brings her thoughtfulness to every interaction, building trust slowly and intentionally. "It's a people business. You have to like people. You have to listen. And you have to show them that you care," she says. "If they feel that, the business will come—maybe not immediately, but eventually."

Broader Networks Lead to Better Leadership

Rosalind Fahey Kruse is a partner in the Corporate & Financial Services Department at Willkie Farr & Gallagher LLP. She serves as the Managing Partner of the firm's New York office and is a member of Willkie's Executive Committee.

Roz believes that effective leadership—and innovation—depends on engaging with people outside your immediate professional circle. She actively participates in broader networks like the Dartmouth Centennial Circle, Women in M&A, and an ongoing roundtable of managing partners in New York. These groups provide more than camaraderie; they're a source of practical insight. "The legal industry tends to maybe lag a little bit behind some other industries in terms of innovation," she says. "I think it is very helpful for us to talk to people in other industries and to just talk about what we're doing."

Whether it's hearing how an accounting firm redesigned its workspace or discussing challenges with other law firm leaders, Roz values the candid, generous exchange of ideas.

"Senior women do share their experiences and share a lot of good information," she says. "That kind of networking has worked very well for me." For Roz, leadership is about more than legal acumen—it's about listening, learning, and staying connected to what's evolving around you.

Association dues are often expensive, and law firms may not be able to afford the cost of their lawyers' memberships. If you are a sole practitioner, the price might come directly out of your pocket, in which case you might be tempted to give joining a second thought.

Join an association if one of the following is true: One, you think you will gain knowledge from the association, which will be helpful in how you do your job, or two, you will meet people who might give you either business or referrals. Litigators are often referred cases by other litigators when there is a conflict, so involvement in the right association can be very helpful. Having said that, the value of effort is multiplied when the lawyer is involved and active in the association and takes on roles on committees and task forces.

The best way to build contacts once you have that membership is to connect with people, get to know them and work with them on a committee or task force. It gives others a chance to see your work and how you think in real time.

Early Networks and Lifelong Connections

There are all kinds of networks that can make a difference in our lives, and some of those networks go back to childhood.

Ellen Holloman, a partner at Kaplan Martin, shared that her early exposure to networking and relationship-building began long before she entered the legal profession. Growing up in New York City's African-American community, Ellen's parents emphasized the importance of social grace, presentation, and personal connection.

When Ellen was just five years old, her parents enrolled her in Jack and Jill of America, a leadership organization for African-American mothers and their children that focused on preparing children for success. Through the club, Ellen learned how to navigate formal environments—like using the right silverware at a fancy restaurant or speaking respectfully with adults. These lessons weren't presented as "networking" at the time, but they laid the foundation for understanding how to build and maintain meaningful relationships across her life.

Ellen explained that the Jack and Jill experience underscored the long-game nature of business development: the idea that you are building your network and reputation long before you need to "use" it. Many of the people she knew in grade school or high school have stayed in her life and now hold positions of influence. Many of the relationships she built in her youth—based on a shared experience, trust, and mutual support—blossomed years later into professional opportunities. "It's not just LinkedIn," she emphasized.

"This is part of your whole life. It's about remembering people, celebrating their lives, and staying in touch."

Her reflections serve as a powerful reminder that the seeds of business development are often planted in childhood—and that authenticity and connection are central to long-term success.

Lise Lotte Hjerrild, Senior Partner at Horten, the prestigious Danish law firm, is former Chair of the IBA Women Lawyers' Committee and now serves on the Management Board of the IBA. With thousands of names in her contact list and a stellar reputation, one of the most powerful lessons she has learned in her career is that networking works best when it's both intentional and long-term. She recounts the story of a standout M&A transaction—a U.S. corporation seeking a deal in Denmark—that came together because of two independent referrals from lawyers at two different firms, each in a different country, whom she had met years earlier. "You never know where a referral is going to come from," she says.

"I try to do at least one business development-related thing each day—whether it's reaching out to someone, participating in an event, or posting something on LinkedIn."

—Lise Lotte Hjerrild

"Somctimes it's someone you helped out with no expectation. That unpredictability is exactly what makes it so valuable." To stay connected, Lise Lotte has developed a consistent approach to relationship-building. "I try to do at least one business development-related thing each day—whether it's reaching out to someone, participating in an event, or posting something on LinkedIn," she explains.

Her favorite metaphor for business development? A case of beer. "You always need to have some cold ones ready—but you also have to think about which ones still need to chill," she says with a smile. "The key is to keep moving, keep building, and never let the fridge go empty."

I can recall many years ago meeting with freshly minted partners at one of the country's largest law firms. A week after they made partner, I would ask them to sit down with me to get to know them better, with the objective of seeing how I or my department could help them. Very often, there would be some awkward small talk. Many of them had literally been working away behind closed doors for years and were not comfortable socializing.

After a few minutes, I would ask them who they shared the news with about their partnership decision, in order to learn more about their network of contacts. Generally, they would say they had been very busy for years and hadn't had time to develop a network. This wasn't completely true. There were people they knew from deals or cases they had worked on, but the fact of the matter was that no one had taught them about building relationships or maintaining a network.

Fortunately, times are changing, and law firms are beginning to educate their associates through training to foster professional development and networking. Networking should start early and be maintained throughout a career.

If a firm hasn't stressed the importance of building a network while lawyers are in their early years at a firm, it is making a mistake. An associate could potentially spend seven or eight years in the company of potential clients, building mediocre social skills. The same associate loses touch with people on the client side with whom they've worked. While they are missing out on nurturing these connections, they may also lose touch with many of their law school friends and classmates. Many of these people will eventually move to the client side and become in-house counsel or start companies. These lost connections can impact the associate's ability to build a robust network over time.

How to Build and Maintain Your Network

Wherever you are on this cycle, even if you have not remained in touch with your contacts from the past, there are ways of kickstarting your network. The following exercise can help you to identify who is in your network.

Start by thinking about and writing down:

- the various educational institutions you've attended since high school
- any associations you've ever been a member of, legal or not
- the names of your immediate circle of friends and acquaintances
- the names of the people you've met who share your interests, such as fellow book club friends

You will probably discover that you already have more contacts than you thought.

But where will you get new business? As you think about building out your network, consider how you've gained clients in the past.

Has it been a referral from a prior client?

Has it been a partner in a different practice in your law firm who has given you business?

Examining your past development activities, including what has worked and where businesses originated, is key to building a plan. That doesn't mean it's the only approach, but it does mean it's a good place to start.

Being Intentional

Think about the types of clients that you want to represent. Are they in a particular industry? Is it in a specific practice area or surrounding a notable issue? The closer you can get to identifying the specific industry, practice and issue, the easier it will be to have a laser focus on where you want to build your network.

This isn't to say that your network should be small or overly focused. In *Collaboration: How Leaders Avoid the Traps, Build Common Ground, and Reap Big Results*, Dr. Heidi K. Gardner, Distinguished Fellow at Harvard Law School's Center on the Legal Profession and former professor at Harvard Business School, demonstrates how two lawyers with similar backgrounds and skills fared differently after making it through a recession—the one with a broader, more diverse network did far better.

Having a wide network isn't just about business leads. It also helps you stay on top of what's changing in the market and in society. Business generation can be unpredictable. It could come from an intermediary, like an accountant or consultant who serves the same audience you do, or it might come through a secondary connection from a friend who happens to know someone who needs your kind of legal help. When you focus on building a network, remember to include those who might seem only tangentially connected—they can be just as valuable down the road.

When you're identifying industries that interest you, try to narrow down the specific companies that are most likely to need your expertise. Once you've pinpointed them, make sure you've connected with key contacts at those companies on LinkedIn. And don't just connect—send a thoughtful note introducing yourself and mentioning what you have in common.

As you think about the legal issues you specialize in, ask yourself what types of companies are most likely to encounter those issues. For example, if you're a tax lawyer whose expertise aligns with the challenges faced by family-owned businesses in the United States, it makes sense to focus on U.S.-based family businesses. If you specialize in CFIUS (Committee on Foreign Investment in the United States), your best opportunities might come from non-U.S. companies looking to invest in the United States.

Don't Forget About Referral Sources

A lawyer focused on helping foreign companies navigate U.S. legal issues might get referrals from non-U.S. law firms. In that case, she should be proactive in reaching out to lawyers at firms overseas who handle this type of work and might look to her for guidance. Being active in organizations like the IBA and serving on committees can also help raise her profile.

Don't overlook the power of influencers. Anyone with a teenager knows the sway influencers have on social media—one mention from a TikTok star can send sales of a new makeup brand through the roof. While the legal profession doesn't have influencers in the same way, there are certainly people within the field who are highly influential. They're the ones who might invite you to speak on a panel, quote you in the media, or refer clients your way. It's worth taking the time to think about who those people are—and how you can connect with them.

Finding the People Who Are "Influencers" in the Legal Profession

Think about what programs are held within your industry and who the speakers are. Who is giving the CLE presentations at PLI, or at Legal Week, or other industry forums?

Take time to look at the panels and see which people are having reoccurring appearances. Those people are likely influencers.

Consider who is chairing the various industry programs and ask if they have chaired other programs. Those people are likely influencers.

Think about the people who are on the boards of various industry associations. Those folks are also influencers.

Once you have an idea of who the influencers are within the profession and within the practice, industry, or issue area in which you are involved, consider the best way to get to know them.

While you can always write a letter to introduce yourself, this is yet another area where LinkedIn is very helpful. Be sure to connect with these people or, at a minimum, follow them to see what activity they are involved in. Attend programs where they're speaking and be sure to introduce yourself.

Consider asking them to serve on a panel if they are an appropriate choice. Even if you decide to do nothing with this group of influencers, knowing who they are is essential. You will also want to keep an eye on where they are speaking and what they're writing about. At a minimum, it's an important way to keep current.

In building out your network, think about what value you can provide people and the best ways of remaining in touch.

Newsletters, blogs, and LinkedIn posts are all very useful, and I often recommend that lawyers consider creating such content to supplement their other marketing efforts. The content should be consistent and focused on two or three themes of a lawyer's practice. It has to be relevant and actionable.

But you may want to think about how best to stay in touch in a more personal way that is targeted to the individual.

A wonderful lawyer with whom I worked used to keep a list in his desk drawer with the names of fifteen people. Ten of them were active clients on whom he depended for his flow of business, but five were referral sources whom he wanted to cultivate.

At least once a week, he would look at the list, think about each individual on it, and ask himself, "What have I done to help that person this week?" If he hadn't spoken with them, sent them something or called them with some new information, he would try to do at least one of these three things.

He set up a news alert for each of those fifteen people so that he would be notified anytime they or their companies were in the news. It allowed him to keep up to date on what his clients were concerned with and also to be able to provide advice or just let them know he saw them in the press if it was appropriate.

This method may work for you, or you may want to develop your own system for staying on top of networking. In my own case, I don't keep a physical list inside my top desk drawer, but I do keep an Excel spreadsheet of the companies I've worked with and the people I've met at those firms. Once a month, I review the list and think about if there's anything I can do to help someone. I often invite past or current clients to serve on panels with me or to be a guest on a podcast that I might be hosting or appearing on. I've also asked lawyers to co-write articles with me. Occasionally, I may send them an idea or two of how we can work together, but that's the rarity.

Four out of five times, my contact with them is simply to say, here's an idea, and here's something I can do to help you. For me, that's authentic. But we each need to find our own way to stay in touch and build our network.

Lesley Wan, originally from New Zealand, is a seasoned general counsel who lives in London. In 2013, she became aware of a persistent gap in the professional lives of senior executive women: They lacked a trusted, supportive community. In response, she founded The Eagle Club, a global network designed to boost confidence, create camaraderie, and offer a safe space for women to share success without fear of being cut down—a nod to what she calls the "tall poppy syndrome." "The Eagle Club is a space where women can say, 'I've won this award,' and others respond with genuine congratulations," she says. "There's no bullying, no ego—just a culture of lifting each other up."

The initiative has grown into a powerful force, with chapters across the EU, United States, APAC and the UAE, a WhatsApp-based community, and a vetted Eaglet program for rising stars. Lesley has also launched an Executive Leadership Academy focused on teaching both technical and interpersonal skills because, as she notes, many women don't invest in themselves unless there is a structure to support it.

Lesley is especially passionate about the importance of networking mid-career when many women begin to lose momentum. "You may get married, you have a new home, you focus on your work—and you forget to stay connected," she says. "But that's exactly when you need your network most." She contrasts this with male colleagues, who often gain mentors early in their careers and quickly raise their visibility. For women, cultivating community is not just good for business—it's essential for survival in environments where they're still underrepresented in leadership and decision-making roles. The Eagle Club, in many ways, is a response to that—part haven, part launch pad.

At the heart of successful networking—whether through formal associations or informal connections—is authenticity. It's not about collecting contacts or making a hard sell. It's about showing up, offering value, and genuinely engaging with people over time.

From Deborah Enix-Ross's bold leap into the ABA to Stacy Phillips's warm dinner parties, and from leveraging influencers to cultivating personal connections, the stories in this chapter remind us that networking is less about being transactional and more about being human. It's about finding your own style, staying curious, and giving first. Because, in the end, the strongest networks—and the richest business opportunities—are built on trust, generosity, and real relationships.

Think Piece

The Power of Purposeful Connection

By Bridget Mary McCormack*

If you had told me ten years ago that I would one day lead the American Arbitration Association–International Centre for Dispute Resolution (AAA–ICDR), I might have paused—not because the idea seemed implausible, but because the path wasn't typical. At the time, I served as an Associate Justice of the Michigan Supreme Court, collaborating across government branches, the legal profession, and the people of our state to enhance the Michigan courts' service and access to justice. Even in public service, my network was expansive and diverse. Courts serve everyone, and my professional relationships ranged broadly—from legal aid attorneys and solo practitioners to global law firm leaders and business executives. Building and nurturing this diverse stakeholder network was fundamental to understanding what justice required and was critical to ensuring I could smoothly navigate new roles, such as when I became the court's Chief Justice in 2019. These relationships became the bridges connecting my public service experience directly to my new responsibilities at the AAA–ICDR.

Many of us learn early that "networking" is transactional, or worse, performative. I used to bristle at the term. But real networks aren't shallow ladders. They're ecosystems. And the richest ecosystems are biodiverse. Throughout my career, building a diverse, mission-aligned network has proven the most powerful way to

* Bridget Mary McCormack is President and CEO of the American Arbitration Association–International Centre for Dispute Resolution. She is also a Strategic Advisor to the Future of the Profession Initiative at the University of Pennsylvania Carey Law School. Until the end of 2022, McCormack was Chief Justice of the Michigan Supreme Court, where she championed innovation and the use of technology to improve access to justice.

progress toward varied goals: justice reform, technological innovation, or impactful business development. My network's organizing principle is "who shares this vision, and how can we support one another?"

Some of my most impactful professional relationships began without a specific goal. A casual conversation at a legal innovation summit about AI's potential eventually grew into strategic initiatives that now shape the AAA–ICDR's direction. These informal yet purposeful connections often crystallize into transformative collaborations. They might not appear neatly in CRM systems, but their impact is undeniable.

When I transitioned from the judiciary to lead the AAA–ICDR, I entered a new organizational structure and marketplace but never felt disconnected. The relationships I cultivated over the years spent listening to and collaborating with people dedicated to improving legal systems buoyed me. Connections with legal tech innovators, academics, bar leaders, and businesspeople weren't simply preparatory; they actively energized my transition.

Building such values-driven networks is essential for women lawyers, especially. Too often, women are signaled to think small regarding business development: Build one client at a time, one collaboration at a time. Yet our networks can—and should—be expansive, strategic, and informed by our whole selves. Some of my strongest connections emerged unexpectedly from conversations about everything from access to justice to parenting. More than once, these conversations evolved into speaking opportunities, board invitations, and fruitful collaborations, significantly boosting visibility and impact.

Here's what I've learned—and what I offer women at all stages of their legal careers:

Lead with curiosity. People remember thoughtful questions and notice when you genuinely listen. Authentic curiosity forms the foundation of meaningful connections.

Invest in people before you need them. The ideal moment to build your network isn't during a big transition. It's now. Show up consistently, offer help generously, and share ideas openly. These investments return in ways you can't predict.

Cross boundaries intentionally. Build connections beyond your immediate practice area or firm. Engage in nonprofit boards, policy initiatives, or academic environments. Innovation and opportunity flourish at these intersections.

Practice proactive generosity. Refer others, especially women. Celebrate their achievements publicly. Introduce them to your contacts. Generosity builds deep trust and strengthens your credibility.

Anchor yourself in purpose. Enduring, robust networks grow up from shared values. Whether building a client base or launching a new initiative, clearly articulate and lead with your "why."

Today, as our organization thoughtfully integrates AI into alternative dispute resolution, my network remains integral. I host a podcast convening diverse voices at the intersection of AI and law. I facilitate workshops with arbitrators, in-house counsel, and academics to envision the future. None of this happens in isolation. It occurs because I've invested profoundly in a network that continually inspires bolder thinking and courageous action.

When women build purposeful connections, we transform the profession. Our collective networks are engines of meaningful, lasting progress.

Chapter 7

Asking for the Business

"The beginning is always today."

—Mary Shelley

For many professionals, especially women, asking for business feels uncomfortable. It can make you feel awkward, and at its worst, you may view it as salesy, aggressive or unprofessional. But with the right mindset and practice, it doesn't have to feel that way. With a practical, authentic approach to asking for work, you can cultivate a practice without feeling like a salesperson.

One of the toughest parts of developing business is asking for the business.

Studies by people like Dr. Larry Richards demonstrate that lawyers are likely the least psychologically resilient of the professions.[1] It is a characteristic that shows up time and time again in his work. That means lawyers have a harder time recovering from rejection

1. *See* Dr. Larry Richards, *Herding Cats: The Lawyer Personality Revealed*, LawyerBrain LLC, https://www.lawyerbrain.com/wp-content/uploads/2023/04/caliper_herding_cats.pdf.

and often avoid doing things that feel out of their comfort zone, particularly if it involves risk.

I remember speaking at a law firm partner retreat where I ran a design thinking workshop to encourage a discussion about business development. At the end of the talk, we opened up the forum for questions. One of my favorite questions came from a very successful young partner. He asked, "But if you ask for business and you don't get it, what then?" After pausing a moment and thinking about it, I turned and asked him, "Will it physically hurt?" When he replied that it wouldn't, it opened up the whole conversation about the fear of asking for business. His question was wonderful because it raised an issue that we often think about but rarely discuss. How awkward is it to ask someone for business?

My very first job out of college was at a public relations firm. In those days, you wouldn't send emails to reporters, but you would call them on the phone and pitch your idea for a story. Oftentimes, the reporters wouldn't answer, and you ended up leaving a message on voicemail, other times they would answer but when you started describing the story idea, they would hang up the phone. I quickly learned to be focused with my story ideas and to speak fast and get to the point.

Many young PR professionals at the time found the response from reporters intimidating and eventually decided to pursue other careers. However, what I learned after a while was that the worst thing that could happen in making press calls was that someone might either not answer their phone or hang up on me. But neither of those things would physically hurt me.

With that in mind, I knew it was somewhat of a numbers game. The story I was pitching had to be a good one, and the reporter had to be the right one; someone who would be interested in the story and the story would fit their publication. I knew that I needed to keep trying. Eventually, it got easier, and I think I became better at refining my pitch. Over time, the fear of rejection floated away.

Occasionally, I still speak with a reporter to suggest a story idea. I know that they might not like each one that I offer, but I also know that that's not a reflection on me. Asking for new business is much the same. At first it seems like a high mountain and something that will be a real struggle, but after a while, you get used to the idea that rejection is not personal. Your technique also improves over time.

One of the great things about being in the new business and marketing field is that I have seen hundreds of women practice asking for business, and I've also seen the rewards that come when they get it. Not every ask will turn into business, and that's okay. Again, it's a numbers game. I think of the wonderful old New York State Lotto slogan, "You need to be in it to win it." And I think that's true with asking for business. If you don't try, you won't get it.

Why We Are Uncomfortable Asking for Business

One reason it's uncomfortable for many lawyers to ask for a piece of business is that they simply lack the training. Most law schools offer very little training or education on the business aspects of a practice, such as client development, managing a firm, establishing a network, or talking about fees—although some law schools are offering education around the edges of the topic, including University of Pennsylvania Carey Law School, Fordham Law School and Cornell Law School. Nevertheless, sales training is the furthest thing from most law students' minds.

To many lawyers, it feels unprofessional to make the ask. I have heard these refrains a hundred times: "I didn't go to law school to do this type of thing." My other favorite, "Law is a profession, and I don't want to sell."

The Basics, Including How to Discuss Fees

Times have changed. Everyone needs to know the basics of how to promote an idea and sell, whether that means making an argument before a judge, presenting an idea to your firm's management or selling your services to a potential client.

Many lawyers don't want to sell because they want to avoid the question of pricing. The fear of having this conversation is a very real issue. If firms have not given lawyers the tools to understand why their billing rates or project fees are what they are, and there has not been a discussion as to what value lawyers bring to their clients, lawyers will feel uncomfortable. Prior to entering a pitch meeting, you should have an idea of the questions that may be posed regarding pricing and be prepared to answer them.

Keep in mind that no one can force your hand if you don't let them. If after having an initial conversation about fees, you are uncomfortable discussing the possibility of offering discounts, it's easy to say, "I will get back to you with additional details."

Instead of making empty promises, you might say, "That's really helpful. I'm going to go back and talk to some colleagues who specialize in pricing. There may be opportunities to provide greater cost consistency, bundle discounts, or even rethink how certain work is being staffed."

Maybe the client is using a white-shoe firm for routine repetitive work and it may be something a less costly firm could handle more efficiently. The point is that the best rainmakers engage, probe, and offer thoughtful solutions. Those solutions don't have to be presented at a first meeting, but asking the right questions is always helpful.

It Doesn't Have to Feel Like Selling

Samantha (Sam) McKenna is known as the guru of all things LinkedIn enterprise sales, and a super salesperson herself. She is the founder of #samsales and a former LinkedIn executive.

Sam believes that one of the most powerful lessons anyone should learn is how to approach new business. For many professionals—especially those in law—even the phrase "asking for the business" can feel awkward or overly aggressive. Sam's advice is to start by thinking about the words you use. She suggests shifting your language to more natural and client-focused wording.

"You're offering support.
That changes the dynamic entirely."

—Samantha McKenna

"I try to never say, 'What are the next steps?' 'Next steps' sounds salesy to me," she explained. "Instead, I always say, 'How can I best support you in our efforts to work together?'"

That small change turns a transactional moment into a much more collaborative one. Rather than positioning yourself as someone pushing a sale, you're offering help. And that's far more comfortable for both parties—especially for lawyers on the asking side who aren't trained in traditional sales.

Sam points out that many professionals fall into the trap of conducting a great client meeting or lunch, only to leave things vague because they don't know how to pivot to make a business ask.

"We're so accustomed to going to lunch with prospective clients, talking about their challenges, nodding along—and then just paying the bill and leaving," she said. "You don't need to close like a salesperson. You just need to ask, 'What would be the best way forward? How can I help you?'"

Sam's favorite phrases, "How can I best support you?" and "How can I help you?" are intentionally open ended and service oriented. They invite the other person to name what they need, whether that's a follow-up call, a formal proposal, or simply time to think.

Importantly, it keeps the door open while avoiding pressure.

You're not saying, "Are you ready to hire me now?" As Sam points out, "You're offering support. That changes the dynamic entirely."

It's a subtle shift, but one that makes all the difference, especially for lawyers trying to build authentic relationships while also growing their books of business.

Find and rehearse the language that is comfortable for you. If you agree that you are providing your legal expertise as a way to deliver help or assist someone or their organization, why not use the words, "I would like to help you" or "What can I do to help you?"

As with any presentation, practice in front of a mirror or record yourself on your phone and play it back for a rehearsal. These steps really do help. In addition, the more often you try asking for business, the more comfortable it will become and the better you will get at doing it.

It's helpful to see how other professionals at the top of their craft have applied Sam's perspective.

Mary Wilson, a partner at Dentons, echoes the sentiment that business development doesn't have to feel like selling.

Instead of hard asks, Mary says she prefers "soft pitches," framing her outreach in terms of helping the client. "What I do is a small part of what they worry about. When they have a financing issue, I'm actually helpful." She'll often offer informal calls to share what she's been seeing in the market. "Even if you just want to talk it through, I'd love to help." That framing allows her to pitch in a way that's aligned with her expertise, confidence, and desire to support clients.

Building Relationships Over Time

For many women, speaking about their own accomplishments feels strange. We shy away from self-promotion. It makes us uncomfortable, and we sometimes see talking about our accomplishments as a negative thing.

Still, to have gotten where you are today, you need to have had a certain amount of grit and ability to handle some self-promotion.

When it comes to building relationships, success likely doesn't come immediately. I often turn to the metaphor of growing a garden. You plant a variety of seeds, continue to nurture them, and one day, after much hard work, you will see some of them flourish. It takes time and patience. Not all of them will sprout, yet you continue to tend the garden. Others use a host of other metaphors to help describe the sales cycle.

Raised in Botswana and Ghana, Naana Frimpong is a Partner and Co-Chair of the US-Africa Practice at DLA Piper and serves as the Honorary Consul for the Republic of Botswana. Her career path has spanned government service, global law firms, and high-stakes international matters. But her approach to business development is deeply human—and deeply rooted in patience, perspective, and personal integrity.

One of the most powerful metaphors she shared reminds me of my own gardening approach to business development. It came from a story her brother once told her about a massive transportation hub being built in a large U.S. city.

"For three years, you'd pass by and see what looked like nothing was happening. People would wonder, what are they really doing? But underground, they were laying the foundation—wiring, plumbing, infrastructure. And then suddenly, the project was up, layered underground with shops and restaurants. All of it looked like it appeared overnight. But all the hard work had been invisible."

To Naana, that project became a symbol for her own business development journey.

"That's how I think about building a practice," Naana told me. "The work often isn't visible—early conversations, small check-ins, thoughtful touches—but it's critical. The foundation takes time. And when it's solid, that's when the real growth becomes possible."

Her story is a reminder that for many women—especially women of color working in elite legal environments—progress may not always look linear. But with intention, relationships, and quiet persistence, that invisible groundwork becomes the very thing that supports long-term success.

Donna Wilson is the Chief Executive Officer and Managing Partner of Manatt, Phelps & Phillips and one of the country's fiercest litigators.

As a young lawyer, prior to joining Manatt, Donna built up a multi-million-dollar practice in California without even having a California office. "I was literally working out of a rental car—with a printer in the trunk and boxes in the back seat. I'd call clients and say, "I'm in the area," and I was—in a sense! I just didn't have a fixed address."

Donna thought to herself, what do I have that is unique in this market that puts me in a place to ask for business? One of those attributes is the fact that she had clerked for a Ninth Circuit judge. "I leaned into those things, befriended people and leveraged every advantage I could. I built a strong book of business because I knew I had to hustle."

"I'm not just here to solve one legal dispute. I am here to build partnerships. I will ask, 'Tell me about your business. Tell me about you. Tell me about what you're worried about.' Once I know those things, I can begin to build a relationship. I will see something in the news and give a potential client a heads-up or find other ways to help them." Donna believes that lawyers can build relationships by demonstrating that they can be a trusted advisor and resource to their clients.

Donna believes that building a network and practice comes down to two words: hustle and consistency. "Those two words, hustle and consistency, are not rocket science. They mean showing up, following through, doing great work—even when no one is watching." Donna goes on, "I say that not as someone who always had it figured out. I remember being a young associate and thinking, 'I'll never be like those partners—they know everyone, they say all the right things, they're so polished.' I truly thought I'd never get there."

And then one day Donna realized, "Wait a second. I now know a lot of people. I've built client relationships. I am doing it."

Donna points out, "When you are younger, building a practice feels completely out of reach. That's why I always say: Don't be intimidated. If you hustle and you're consistent, it takes you a long way. That's how relationships are built."

Building client relationships involves a lot of work. It involves deeply understanding a potential client's business and being consistent. The reality is that building those relationships requires time. The through line with all of these women, Sam, Naana, and Donna, is that they created connections that were built over decades. The jump to asking for business doesn't happen overnight.

Confident Approaches

Natasha Harrison left her role as Deputy Chair of Boies Schiller Flexner in 2022 to launch a new firm. Today, she is the founder and Managing Partner of Pallas Partners, an elite litigation and disputes firm based in London and New York.

Natasha has a direct and confident approach to business development that is deeply rooted in her upbringing. Raised in an immigrant working-class family—her father from Greece and her mother from Ireland—she learned early on that nothing would be handed to her. "I had to ask for everything: internships, jobs, opportunities. Nothing came easily to me," she recalls. "So, I got used to it. I always say that the worst someone can say is 'no.' But they'll still remember you."

That mindset served her not only as a successful litigator but as an entrepreneur. When she launched Pallas Partners, she wasn't just building a practice—she was building an institution from the ground up. Armed with a blank sheet of paper and a vision for what a modern, values-driven law firm could look like, she designed every element intentionally: from the firm's name (inspired by Pallas Athena, goddess of wisdom and war), to its inclusive culture and fee structures that align with client needs.

But launching the firm also meant doubling down on the same relationship-building and sales skills she had developed early in her career. As she described it, "asking, reaching out, and building."

"At three o'clock in the morning on launch day, I thought, 'I can't believe, I've started a law firm.'" But the risk paid off. Her longtime clients followed her. Her team followed her. New clients were drawn to the clarity of her vision and her deep understanding of the business challenges they faced. She could not afford to be shy or have trepidation about asking clients to come with her.

Owning her own firm has only strengthened her approach. "Clients now see me differently," she says. "They know I understand what it means to be a founder and build a business. That trust opens new doors—and allows me to sit with them not just as a litigator, but as a strategic advisor."

Her advice for others, especially women who hesitate to ask for business, is simple: "Don't wait. Don't be afraid to ask. You're not going to get everything. And yet often, that's where it starts."

Building a new firm is a challenge and so is continuing to build one where cross-border work is essential. Ingrid Pierce is the Global Managing Partner of Walkers, a leading international law firm with its roots in the Cayman Islands. Along with her talent and great relationship building skills, she has built a remarkable career advising investment managers, trustees, and fiduciaries on structuring their products. She has also developed a sharp instinct for how to lead, mentor, and grow a business.

"If you think you don't have the time to build a relationship and you want the work, then you just have to put on your superwoman outfit and get over yourself and ask."

—Ingrid Pierce

When it comes to the art of asking for work, Ingrid is frank. "It was anathema when I started out. No one would even hand out business cards." But she's also practical. Today, she tells younger female lawyers that asking for business isn't about being pushy, it's about being strategic and self-aware. "If you think you don't have the time to build a relationship and you want the work, then you just have to put on your superwoman outfit, get over yourself and ask."

That said, Ingrid is quick to note that business development is not one-size-fits-all. "You don't have to be the outgoing person who goes to the conference or goes on the road," she says. "If you're a whiz at desktop marketing, then do that."

Her message is empowering. Success doesn't come from adopting someone else's voice—it comes from leaning into your own. Whether it's speaking on panels, writing thought leadership, or connecting one-on-one with peers, she believes everyone can find a path that feels natural and gets positive results.

Ingrid's advice for women, in particular, is to stop apologizing for doing it differently. There's no gold standard for business development—just what works for you. "The key is to be curious and be interested in your industry," she says. "If you care about your clients, and if you want to learn more about what they do, the business will follow."

It's a simple principle but one that has guided Ingrid through both client success and leadership roles, and it's a reminder that building a book of business doesn't require bravado—just thoughtful, consistent engagement in your own style.

Adding the Value

Like any skill, asking for business gets easier with practice. The key is to keep the ask pressure-free—and think of it as adding value when there's already a strong relationship in place. The conversation feels natural rather than transactional.

Responsiveness also goes a long way; being quick and helpful signals that you'll care enough in the relationship to make the other person look good. It's an approach that builds trust and goodwill.

According to Annalisa Reale, business is built on relationships and having empathy for your client. "When you and a client establish a connection and mutual respect, they will seek out business on their terms—whether in banking, finance, or any other field. It helps to put yourself in their shoes."

> "When you and a client establish a connection and mutual respect, they will seek out business on their terms—whether in banking, finance, or any other field. It helps to put yourself in their shoes."
>
> **—Annalisa Reale**

One approach to consider is to offer to take on a small assignment. Of course, make sure to seek guidance from your firm and confirm there are no conflicts. Still, this is a great way to show initiative.

Annalisa also suggests another method: offer to make introductions to others at your firm and ask if you can sit in on the conversation. This can be an effective way to start building more significant multi-practice relationships with several pathways into a client.

"When you bring value, asking to be hired doesn't feel like a favor—it feels like a win-win. If you've built a genuine relationship with a potential client and you know you can help them, it's not such a big ask."

—Dominique Hussey

Dominique Hussey is the Chief Executive at Bennett Jones, a Canadian based law firm, serving clients with complex, high-stakes matters across Canada and internationally. Dominique leads the firm's Intellectual Property Litigation group and serves as co-head of its Innovation, Technology, and Branding group. She has a substantial book of business and is an impressive lawyer and rainmaker. Dominique believes strongly that the approach to developing a client should be based on providing great value.

According to Dominique, "When you bring value, asking to be hired doesn't feel like asking for a favor—it feels like a win-win. If you've built a genuine relationship with a potential client and you know you can help them, it's not such a big ask."

Simple phrasing like "I'd love to work together if something comes up" or "I'd be very interested in helping with that" can open the door without making anyone uncomfortable."If the ask involves real help and value, it's an easier ask.

Managing Nerves

Just like stepping on stage to give a speech, asking for business can make people nervous.

As Franklin Roosevelt said, "the only thing we have to fear is fear itself." But managing anxiety around business development and specifically making the ask for business is easier said than done. There are techniques, however, to help you break the cycle of perpetuating nervousness.

Jennifer Kupferman is a former Big Law attorney turned therapist who now works extensively with lawyers, particularly women. She explains the power of "grounding exercises" to help a lawyer reconnect with the present moment, especially during times of anxiety, stress, or overwhelming emotions. These exercises can help both body and mind by creating a sense of stability and calm. "When we're stressed about something, we often replay the worst-case scenario in our heads," she says. "But there are techniques that help shift our physiological state and create space for a clearer, calmer mindset. Grounding exercises are perfect for this."

Kupferman recommends the physiological sigh, a breathing method that involves two short inhales through the nose followed by a long exhale through the mouth. "It mimics what your body already does when you're sobbing—this is how the body gives itself relief and completes the stress cycle," she explains. She also suggests using other evidence-based practices, such as humming or holding an ice cube in your hand to activate the vagus nerve and bring the nervous system back to a regulated state. These simple but powerful tools can help lawyers feel more centered before a pitch—transforming what feels threatening into something far more manageable.

I am also an admirer of Dr. Amy Cuddy's work which tells women that it's important to take a moment before a big presentation or meeting, find a quiet spot and practice which she calls power posing.[2] By literally reaching out one's arms in whatever way seems comfortable and assuming the proper straight posture, it helps you take up space and feel larger than life. In many ways, holding that pose for a few moments can help boost your confidence.

While Amy's work has been controversial, believing in oneself and taking a breath, whether in a power pose or a moment of calm before a presentation, is an enormous help in how we face the world.

To calm nerves or mitigate imposter syndrome, I often also suggest to lawyers that they think about their past successes and list them in their head or write them down on a piece of paper. With that information top of mind, they can become more confident. And if the situation is a formal pitch for work, chances are the lawyer has been invited to pitch, suggesting that the lawyer has a strong case for being in the spot she finds herself in.

Focusing on the Existing Client

How well do you know your clients? By getting to know them even better, you'll be better equipped to serve them on a daily basis and to become a close, trusted advisor. It will also become easier to say, "How can I help you?" once you know what is on their plate.

You've probably often heard that the best source of business is an existing client. Studies have shown that it is much more expensive to generate a brand-new piece of business than to garner new business from an existing client.[3]

Part of building a strong network involves strengthening those contacts that you already have. By viewing clients more as people and less as an "account" or "the client," you'll naturally strengthen

---

2. *See* Amy J. C. Cuddy, S. Jack Schultz & Nathan E. Fosse, *P-curving a more comprehensive body of research on postural feedback reveals clear evidential value for power-posing effects: Reply to Simmons and Simonsohn (2017)*, 29(4) Psych. Sci. 656 (2018), https://doi.org/10.1177/0956797617746749.
3. *See* Fred Reichheld, *Prescription for Cutting Costs*, Bain & Co. (Oct. 2001), https://www.bain.com/insights/prescription-for-cutting-costs-bain-brief/.

the relationship. Clients hate to be seen as transactional cash registers for their outside lawyers. Most in-house counsel want lawyers who go the extra step and work to build a relationship.

If you provide outstanding service to your clients today, they may look to you to handle additional work for their company and become your best referral source for new clients in the future.

Take Culture into Account

Culture plays a big role, not just from one firm to another, but from one region of the world to another.

Sara Koleilat-Aranjo's cross-border experience has given her a deep appreciation for cultural nuance, especially when it comes to developing business.

"You don't engage the same way with someone from the Middle East as you do to someone from Europe or the U.S.," she explains. In the Gulf, she notes, building trust is personal, incremental, and sometimes even a test of character. "You have to create a link. It takes weeks, sometimes months or even years. And if you push too fast, it backfires." She contrasts this with Western markets where transactional speed is valued, adding, "The best strategy is sometimes no strategy—just be genuine, patient, and aware of where the other person is coming from."

Sara's understanding of cultural context is not theoretical—it's rooted in lived experience and refined through practical application. At business school in France, she studied cross-cultural management. She later applied those lessons while working at a global bank during the 2008 financial crisis, advising clients ranging from royals to government leaders. "You're not just managing transactions; you're managing relationships," she says.

As a senior international arbitration lawyer in the Middle East, she constantly adjusts her communication style to suit the nationality, gender, and individual background of her audience. "Today,

I was speaking to a client in Switzerland. I wouldn't speak to them the same way I speak to someone from Dubai."

Her advice to others: Don't fake connection or rush rapport. "If you sit down and immediately try to pitch, they'll smile politely and walk away. But if you're genuinely interested—if you listen and learn about their business and culture—you'll build something meaningful. Some of my clients are now good friends."

Showing Gratitude and Interest

Alison Jeffrey is Senior Advisor, Strategic Initiatives and Client Development Coach at Blakes, one of Canada's premier business law firms. She believes that a great approach to promoting your expertise when you are in a new business situation is to frame your prior work with gratitude and recognition of others.

"For example, instead of saying nothing about your role in a big case, you might say: 'I was delighted when Partner X asked me to lead this litigation. It's going well—we've had a couple of early wins, and I have a fantastic team. Senior Associate X has been phenomenal, and I'm grateful to be leading such a strong group.'"

Alison points out that in this way, you're acknowledging your leadership while also giving credit to the team. "You're not boasting—you're sharing a success. And that's something we should all get better at doing."

"You're not boasting—you're sharing a success. And that's something we should all get better at doing."

—Alison Jeffrey

Great rainmakers ask questions not just out of curiosity, but because they genuinely care and have empathy. According to Adam Severson of Baker Donelson, "Take, for example, a general counsel who says, 'I've been given a goal to reduce my legal spend by 12%.' Some people—those who aren't the best rainmakers—might respond with, 'Oh, okay . . . What are your plans for the holidays?'"

"But a skilled rainmaker, someone who is truly listening and understands both the business of law and their firm's capabilities, would take a different approach. They might ask, 'As you think about that goal, do you see any low-hanging fruit for cost-cutting? What processes are you putting in place to achieve those savings? Will technology play a role? Is this strictly about overall legal spending, or does it also involve headcount?'"

From there, the conversation naturally deepens. A thoughtful rainmaker keeps asking, uncovering the real challenges behind that goal. And yes, that could turn into a thirty-minute discussion about reducing legal spending by 12%. But in doing it, they get much closer to becoming that coveted trusted advisor.

For each of your clients, you should be able to review the Client-Relationship Health Diagnostic™ and know the answers to the questions. This is something I've often used with my own firm and individual clients.

General Assessment

- How did they come to you or the firm?
- Was a referral source involved in their hiring the firm, and if so, who was that?
- How long have they used the firm, and what have their billings/realization been year-to-year?
- Are there several firm contacts at the client or just one?
- Who are their various contacts at the firm?

Satisfaction and Nurturing the Relationship

- How do they define success?
- What do you think can make them say, "Wow, I would never leave them?"
- What can be done to improve and feed the connection?

Threats to the Relationship

- What keeps them up at night?
- What other law firms are they using, and for what purpose?
- Are there succession issues on either the client or the firm side?
- Have they ever had a problem with the firm's work or any conflicts or other disagreements?

Feeding the Connection

- What do you know about your client's life outside of work?
- When was the last time you saw them?
- When was the last time they were at your office?
- What industry events and associations are important to them?

Internal Structure

- To whom do they report?
- How are they evaluated?
- Who reports to them?
- How much time does it take them in terms of training their staff?
- What are their own business goals? (e.g. promotion, adding to staff, leaving the company)

Ongoing Communication

- How important is it to update them with information?
- How do they like to receive that information?
- What system do you have for staying in touch with them?
- What are you doing to keep abreast of changes in their business and their industry?

Diagnostic Discussion

- What steps can be taken to strengthen and grow the relationship?
- What are the long-term objectives to grow the client?
- What are the short-term objectives to grow the client?
- What are three short-term steps you can take this month to improve the relationship?

There are ways to explore the art of asking for business without feeling awkward or pushy—from Sam McKenna's simple shift in phrasing to Mary Wilson's "soft pitch" approach and Natasha Harrison's bold confidence. We can see how leading women lawyers build authentic relationships and position themselves as trusted advisors.

Through stories of grit and grace—from Donna Wilson's hustle to Naana Frimpong's foundation metaphor and Ingrid Pierce's mindset shift—we learn that asking for business is less about closing a deal and more about offering value, support, and strategic insight. The key message is clear: Find your voice, offer genuine value, and just ask.

Think Piece

What If Asking for Business Isn't Really About "Selling" at All?

By Dr. Heidi K. Gardner*

For many lawyers—especially women—the idea of asking for business feels uncomfortable. Legal training emphasizes precision and technical mastery, not the kinds of conversations that drive client growth. Add to that the lingering stigma around "selling" as pushy or self-serving, and it's no wonder these conversations often get avoided.

But what if we've misunderstood the task?

What if asking for business isn't about self-promotion—but about teaming up with clients to solve their toughest challenges?

That's the mindset shift. And it's one we've seen transform client relationships and unlock real growth—for firms and individuals alike.

Start with the Right Mindframe: You're Solving, Not Selling

This shift is essential: women negotiate more confidently when advocating on behalf of others, according to research by economist Linda Babcock. The same principle applies here. Instead of viewing

* Heidi K. Gardner, Ph.D. is a Distinguished Fellow at Harvard Law School and a former professor at Harvard Business School. She also serves as faculty chair and instructor for multiple executive education programs at both institutions. A globally recognized advisor, keynote speaker, and facilitator, Dr. Gardner works with organizations across many industries to elevate performance through stronger collaboration and leadership. Named by Thinkers50 as a Next Generation Business Guru and one of the world's top leadership experts, she is CEO of the research and advisory firm Gardner & Co.

business development as a personal ask, view it as helping the client succeed—and spotlighting your colleagues who can deliver that success.

As one GC told us, "When a lawyer brings in a colleague with deep expertise, it shows they're invested in my success—not just their own book of business."

This reframe shifts the focus outward. You're not selfishly pushing services. You're spotting needs and connecting the client to people who can help.

Why This Works: Clients Want (and Reward) Collaboration

Let's ground this thesis in data. Over the past decade, we've interviewed hundreds of GCs, board members, heads of procurement, and other corporate leaders through our work at Gardner & Co. and more recently Smarter Collaboration International. Across industries and geographies, they're saying the same thing:

> "I don't have legal problems. I have problem problems."

In a VUCA world—volatile, uncertain, complex, and ambiguous—clients want more than isolated expertise. They want outside counsel who can integrate multiple perspectives, anticipate their needs, and help them move quickly and wisely.

Clients reward that kind of collaboration. Consider:

- At one global law firm, 90% of clients served by multiple partners said they would stay with the firm if their lead partner left—compared to just 28% of clients served by a single partner.
- Multi-practice clients generate significantly more revenue—and the impact is more than additive. A client served by three practices often brings in far more revenue

than three separate, single-practice clients combined. This finding demonstrates that clients *value* broader service; it benefits them, so they're willing to pay.

- Profitability tends to rise over time. While fee pressure may increase early in a collaborative relationship, **discounting levels off** as the client becomes more embedded and sees the value.
- And here's the kicker: most firms still underperform on this front. In one representative firm, **over half of clients were served by just one partner**—despite clear evidence that multi-partner relationships drive loyalty and growth.

Beyond the numbers, collaboration delivers value that clients feel:

- **Access to the firm's best minds.** Clients expect you to bring in experts—not pretend you know it all.
- **Business insights.** Cross-functional teams often surface patterns or opportunities the client hadn't noticed.
- **Benchmarking.** "If you can tell me just one thing my competitor is doing better, I'll give you all the time in the world," one GC said.
- **Innovation.** Diverse teams generate more creative, tailored solutions—especially important for novel or evolving challenges.
- **Efficiency.** True experts solve problems faster and more cost-effectively.
- **Simplicity.** Clients increasingly favor firms that can serve as "core providers," streamlining their vendor base.

Not every client values these factors equally, but understanding your client's value drivers gives you the edge to position collaboration in a way that resonates with their needs.

Once You're Ready: A Practical Roadmap

With the right mindset and the clear case for collaboration, here's a simple three-step roadmap to take thoughtful action:

1. *Develop a Hypothesis*

Before reaching out, do your homework. What's likely on the client's radar—regulatory changes, geographic expansion, ESG demands?

Come prepared with a point of view. One GC told us, "It's downright refreshing when a lawyer spots an issue before I even know it's headed my way." Showing up with foresight sets you apart—and shows you're thinking strategically.

Bonus stat: In our work with hundreds of GCs, the ones most loyal to their firms consistently cited this kind of "anticipatory thinking" as a key differentiator.

2. *Frame It As a Client Insights Meeting*

Skip the pitch. Instead, create space for dialogue. Position the meeting as a way to better understand their current goals and challenges.

Ask open-ended questions like:

- "What's an issue that keeps getting pushed down your to-do list?"
- "What regulatory or stakeholder pressures are you anticipating in the next six to twelve months?"
- "Where could outside perspective help your team think differently?"

Clients don't want a sales call. They want a sounding board—and a thought partner.

3. Make the Ask About Others

Use your insights to connect the client with someone in your firm who's uniquely positioned to help. Broadening the resources available to them reinforces your role as a strategic partner focused on their most important goals.

Consider this example:

During a check-in, Emily, a partner at a mid-size firm, asked her pharma client, "What's your biggest headache as you expand into new markets?" The client flagged regulatory overload across jurisdictions.

Emily introduced Raj, her go-to colleague for compliance strategy. That led to a joint workshop that pinpointed efficiencies and saved the client time and resources. The client's VP later said, "I'd never have connected with Raj if Emily hadn't seen the bigger picture."

That's how you move from talking fees to delivering results.

Bottom Line

Asking for business doesn't have to feel transactional. Using our Smarter Collaboration Business Development methodology, Gardner & Co. coaches work with lawyers to hone their client growth approach. We consistently find that lawyers who reframe the "ask" as "client advocacy" are more successful at engaging the right expertise and maintaining a problem-solving focus. Ultimately, they build deeper trust and stronger partnerships that result in quantifiable business success.

The data backs it up. The outcomes prove it. And clients are asking for it—explicitly.

So go ahead. Start the conversation. Not because you're trying to "sell," but because you're ready to help.

Chapter 8

The Business Development Mindset: Learning from Others and Developing Grit

"There are two ways of spreading light:
to be the candle or the mirror that reflects it."

—Edith Wharton

We are all connected, whether we are the candle (the mentor) or the mirror (the mentee). Mentoring, building relationships and personal growth are interconnected issues that combine to help formulate a business development mindset.

How the Examples of Others Can Help You Develop Your Rainmaking Skills

Mentors

Mentors are individuals who guide us by showing us the way, demonstrating behavior for us to emulate. If they are truly exceptional, they may become sponsors, those rare individuals who ensure that you are included in significant conversations and involved in activities that will truly benefit your career.

When I first started at Debevoise & Plimpton, M&A partner and private equity guru Franci Blassberg introduced herself to me during my first week at the firm. She invited me to coffee and explained the steps I needed to succeed at Debevoise. While she was a mentor, she was also a sponsor, and brought me to practice group meetings, introducing me at various partner discussions and including me in management committee gatherings.

At Cravath, Evan Chesler and Allen Parker were two of my mentors. They both went the distance to ensure I succeeded. They invited me in for management conversations and involved me in strategic decision-making.

Mentors come in all kinds of shapes and sizes and different forms of packaging. Mentors may be women or men. They may be older or younger. Sometimes, we search them out; other times, they find us.

Kaplan Martin's Ellen Holloman credits much of her enormous success as a lawyer and rainmaker to the guidance of thoughtful mentors—most notably Stephen Fraidin, a corporate partner at Cadwalader. Though not a litigator like Ellen, Steven became a pivotal figure in Ellen's career during her years at Cadwalader, offering perspective, not just on legal strategy but on how to think more like a businessperson. "He never sugarcoated feedback but delivered it in a way that made me feel inspired rather than diminished."

Steven's mentorship helped Ellen grow in her confidence and, ultimately, in her approach to client development. He encouraged her to view developing business as an authentic extension of who she was—by suggesting she build relationships naturally, over lunch or coffee. He also suggested that she wait until the end of the conversation to say, "I'd love to work with you." That approach, she said, felt genuine and human, and it has stuck with her.

And the great thing about mentors is that there is no limit on how many you may have during your career.

Ellen described the importance of having a "personal board of directors—a mix of mentors, sponsors, and wise advisors who help you navigate the professional world." Ellen emphasized that mentorship doesn't always have to come from an obvious senior person or even someone within your own practice area. What matters is their insight and willingness to invest in your growth.

For women, and especially women of color, this kind of support is critical. It helps counteract the constant pressure to prove oneself, and it provides a safe space to learn, grow, and course-correct without fear of judgment. Ellen's experience shows how powerful mentorship can be when it's rooted in respect, honesty, and a shared desire to see someone succeed.

There are also mentors who fall higher on the sponsor range, such as the ones I had both at Debevoise and at Cravath, who also take the additional steps of making introductions and giving feedback.

Gayle Klein, Co-head of US litigation, arbitration and global investigations at Freshfields, credits much of her rise to key mentors and sponsors who not only believed in her but actively opened doors.

Ralph Miller, an early mentor during Gayle's time as a Weil Gotshal & Manges associate, made a lasting impact by his offering thoughtful critiques and expressing appreciation for her efforts. "When you're working hard as a lawyer—nights, weekends, time away from your family—it means a lot to have someone tell you that your sacrifices matter," says Gayle. That support helped instill in her a deep commitment to perfecting her craft.

Penny Reid, now a partner at Sidley, was formerly at Weil, where she placed Gayle on significant cases and modeled how to balance life outside of work with a demanding legal career.

Later, Mike McKool of McKool Smith sponsored her into leadership roles at the firm.

These individuals didn't just help Gayle develop her legal skills—they demonstrated how to build practices, and at the same time, elevated her visibility and helped her discover how to lead. Gayle says, "My best mentors—particularly the women—taught me not just how to practice law, but how to be a woman practicing law without apologizing for it."

Vanessa Jackson, a talented partner in Davis Polk's Corporate Finance group, shared that she has learned to intentionally use her identity—as a woman, a mother, and a Black lawyer—as her "game-changer." While some may view these aspects as obstacles in the traditional world of business development, she sees them as assets that allow her to connect more meaningfully with clients and colleagues.

"Wins for me were when people spoke up and advocated for me when I wasn't even in the room."

—Vanessa Jackson

But she is clear that the growth of her profile in the industry didn't happen in isolation. "One thousand percent, it was the mentors," she says, crediting senior partners who gave her not just guidance but access—bringing her into client meetings, pitches, and training sessions. They showed her what business development looks like at the highest level.

Vanessa noted that these opportunities were formative. She absorbed not only how partners spoke to clients but also how they prepared, followed up, and built trust over time. Just as important were the moments she wasn't present, when those mentors advocated for her behind closed doors. "Wins for me were when people spoke up and advocated for me when I wasn't even in the room," she said. "That kind of sponsorship," she emphasized, "can make all the difference for younger lawyers—especially in a high-performing, all-equity partnership like Davis Polk, where visibility and advocacy are essential for long-term success."

Role Models

The greatest issue I see for women lawyers who want to develop business is that many have not seen others do it. We know that there is a disproportionately lower number of women in true leadership positions at law firms, and because of that, there may be fewer opportunities to see others who look or act like us in the role of business developer.

Finding role models is not always a simple thing.

When tax law star Lesley Adamo considered the very real challenges of juggling motherhood and a demanding career in the legal industry, she wondered if long-term success at a law firm could coexist with family. At Lowenstein, she met successful women who had both. During a candid conversation at a women's networking event, she shared her hesitation about starting a family while also approaching partner consideration and building a practice. Lesley said, "A woman partner advised me, 'You just do it. You don't take yourself out of the game. If it becomes unmanageable, you can adjust.'"

"A woman partner advised me, 'You just do it. You don't take yourself out of the game. If it becomes unmanageable, you can adjust.'"

—Lesley Adamo

That moment of mentorship and having role models gave Lesley the confidence to stay at the firm. She got pregnant, went on maternity leave during the first half of the year she was under consideration for partner, and still made partner in that year. "It's so important to meet women who have achieved these milestones," she said. "When you find them within your own firm, it's even more powerful."

Of course, men can and do serve as important role models to female attorneys, just as they serve as important mentors.

Brad Karp, the chairman of Paul Weiss, was my co-chair for the PLI program "Business Development All Stars." Brad has built a litigation practice that is one of the most admired in the profession. His insights served as a masterclass in what it means to create a practice and lead a firm. He teaches young associates that business development is a daily discipline, requiring consistent nurturing.

Brad emphasizes that building a practice is not a mystery; at its core, it's about building genuine relationships, with existing clients, potential clients, and colleagues, especially when you're a junior lawyer. He encourages young associates to take the time to connect with in-house counsel, noting that these may be the people they end up working with for decades.

Learning from Mentors and Role Models but Developing Your Own Style

Tim Diemand is a trial lawyer known for handling high-exposure complex litigation, and today he is the leader of the law firm Wiggin and Dana. Tim believes the most powerful tool in business development is authenticity. In his mentoring of younger lawyers—particularly women—he encourages them not to blindly replicate his business development style or tactics but instead to find their own voice.

"The best advice I've given as a mentor is to be your authentic self," he said. "Don't just parrot what I do. You can learn and take ideas from things that I've done, but if you're not authentic, clients will see that every day." He emphasized that authenticity isn't just a strategic advantage; it's what makes the work sustainable and meaningful. Trying to emulate someone else's persona, he warns, is not only ineffective but will eventually become a burden: "If you're trying to be something you're not, you won't enjoy it."

Tim shared the example of a litigation partner, a colleague whose personality is, as he puts it, "like night and day" compared to his own. "I've said to her, don't be like me—that's not you," he recalled. And for her to hear that is great. "She knows, 'I can be myself and be successful. I don't have to parrot what Tim does,' and it's been great to watch her flourish with her own personality and approach."

Tim believes that role models are important but not as templates to copy—instead, they should inspire younger lawyers to believe that there is more than one path to success. As the profession continues to evolve and more women rise into leadership roles, Tim is heartened by the increasing diversity of styles that allows younger lawyers to now be inspired in different ways.

Inspiration from Other Industries

While there is no shortage of great ideas and new developments coming out of law firms when it comes to business development, it is essential to also look beyond our own industry. Some of the greatest inspiration for me personally often comes from businesses *outside* the legal profession.

A friend of mine, Greg Furman, is the founder of the Luxury Marketing Council. Members of the Council include chief marketers and leaders of companies that are in the luxury space, such as Sotheby's, Bergdorf Goodman, and a handful of law firms with IP or Trust and Estates practices for high-worth individuals—the types of people who might frequent Sotheby's or Bergdorf Goodman.

Greg was terrific at teaching me about what he did when he served as CMO at Bergdorf Goodman. Greg shared with me that the company had a laser-like concentration on their top clients, offering them exclusive programs and benefits. I was able to take that back to the firm where I worked at the time and develop a program focusing on our top clients. It wasn't quite the same as Bergdorf Goodman; we wouldn't be offering fashion shows, but we rolled out any new programs to our top clients and focused on them whenever there was an event to provide special seating and other accommodations.

It was an idea that came from another industry, and while it didn't translate precisely, it did inspire us to do something similar. Getting ideas from new organizations or different types of industries can be very helpful.

Ilene Marquardt, now the Head of Legal Engagement for the Client Relationship Group at Wells Fargo Advisors, has carved out a remarkable career by combining deep legal acumen with a strategic business mindset.

With roots in litigation and regulatory enforcement, Ilene began her legal journey at Morgan Lewis, where she quickly gravitated toward the fast-paced world of securities law. From those early days, Ilene followed her instincts, choosing matters that intrigued her, even when they didn't fit the traditional mold. "I was drawn to the work that felt hands-on and engaging—digging into facts, preparing witnesses for testimony, and learning the business behind the law."

As her career progressed—from law firm associate to senior in-house counsel roles at PaineWebber, UBS, and now Wells Fargo—Ilene consistently broadened her scope. She made it a point to say yes to new responsibilities, whether it was contracts, trademarks, or operational risk, all in service of better understanding the businesses she advised. Her efforts paid off when she was asked to serve as Head of Litigation and Regulatory for the retail brokerage group—a role she handled with characteristic calm just as the 2008 financial crisis hit.

But perhaps what stands out most in Ilene's journey is her evolution from being promoted for "just doing her job" to realizing the importance of actively owning her career. A pivotal moment earlier in her career came when she turned down a role out of fear; she wasn't ready—a decision she later regretted deeply. "I was perfectly capable," she reflects. "I should have taken it." That experience shaped her approach moving forward: Speak up, seek growth, and don't let fear get in the way of progressing your career and taking on new challenges.

Today, she mentors others with the same message, telling colleagues, "If you're too comfortable, it's time to move."

Ilene's path is a masterclass in grit and staying open to growth. She built her reputation not by chasing titles but by following her curiosity, deepening her expertise, and learning the art of speaking up—especially when the stakes were high. Her story is a powerful reminder that great careers are rarely linear. They're built by those who position themselves with purpose and own every step along the way.

With accounting firms now offering legal services and management consulting firms stretching across industries, it has become more common for law firms to look at other industries to see what can be learned.

A wonderful lawyer I knew mentioned to me at some point that an accounting firm with which he had started to work had sent him a welcome package. The package included materials about how the accounting firm could help the lawyer.

Inspired by this example, our law firm developed its own new client welcome kit, to be tailored to each client. Once the client was brought into the firm, we would work with the individual partner who was responsible for the engagement and offer a suggested list of items that the firm could provide to the client. Those items could include a list of upcoming webinars that the firm had planned, a description of office space for the client to use when they were visiting New York, and a list of CLE programs that we could tailor and offer to the client in house. We created a customized card with the lawyers' photos and contact information of people who would be working on their matters. While these were simple ideas and ideas that would not cost the firm much extra in dollars, they started the engagement off on a positive note.

What I loved most about this concept was that it was something that came not from another law firm but from an accounting firm. It was one of those ideas that, with a little bit of creativity, we could adapt for use at a law firm.

Linda Orton has worked in professional services marketing for several decades, both as a consultant and as a CMO at these firms. She is adamant that lawyers should not limit their growth strategies to what other law firms are doing. Instead, she encourages lawyers to look beyond the legal profession, drawing inspiration from consumer goods, technology, and consulting. "Professional services firms need to learn best practices from consumer goods and tech," she says. "Lawyers should not be limiting themselves to what other law firms are doing."

For Linda, part of effective business development is about breaking out of the echo chamber. Attending bar association events or legal conferences can be helpful but shouldn't be the sole source of networking or inspiration. "You don't always want to be where all the other lawyers are," she emphasizes.

"You want to be where your potential prospects and clients are." She recommends identifying the industry events, trade groups, or professional spaces where clients—not peers—congregate and showing up there with purpose.

Linda's call to action is clear: Innovation doesn't start with another CLE panel. It starts when lawyers step outside of legal norms, ask questions, and borrow the best ideas—wherever they find them.

Helen Burness is a multitalented marketing professional based in the UK. In Helen's view, the law is one of the few industries still squeamish about the word "sales." "In tech or finance, sales are seen as essential. But in law, people talk around it. They'll say 'relationship-building' or 'client engagement,' but heaven forbid they say 'sales strategy.'"

"When you understand how to sell your value, you stop waiting for someone to 'discover' you. You start building your own path."

—Helen Burness

She believes this discomfort stems from the law's legacy of being advisors people simply sought out for their brilliance, like doctors. But business law is a thriving industry today with competition that comes from all angles. "That model doesn't work anymore. You have to be intentional about winning work—and that means embracing a sales mindset."

She encourages lawyers to take cues from other industries where marketing and business development are integrated disciplines led by professionals. "In law, lawyers often try to run the marketing. In other sectors, marketing runs marketing. That's a huge difference." Ultimately, she believes embracing sales is about control: "When you understand how to sell your value, you stop waiting for someone to 'discover' you. You start building your own path."

Building Visibility and Grit: Growing Through the Challenges

Victoria Reese is a partner at Heidrick & Struggles. She serves on the management team as the Global Managing Partner of the Corporate Officers' Practice. Victoria says, "Women sometimes prioritize other responsibilities over their career aspirations and don't always advocate for themselves. I contacted a female General Counsel to discuss a potential opportunity, and she mentioned that it was her dream job but that she was currently too busy to consider any new positions." Victoria said that while she respected the candidate's response, she followed up the next day to propose a plan. Victoria worked with the candidate to address her timing concerns while allowing her to pursue the role. "She ultimately secured the position and is now thriving."

Research suggests that there may be a notable difference between men and women when it comes to applying for jobs for which they do not meet all the listed qualifications. This disparity highlights support for encouraging more women to pursue opportunities even when they do not meet every listed criterion. According to Victoria, "often, women candidates lead a conversation with me as to why they are not qualified for a job versus why they are qualified."

Grit—What It Is and Why It Matters

Dr. Milana Hogan is the Chief Talent Officer at Sullivan & Cromwell and the author of the book, *Grit: The Secret to Advancement*. She is also a leading voice in the ABA Commission on Women in the Profession. Milana believes that grit—the combination of passion and perseverance over time—is not only essential for legal success but especially transformative for women navigating the challenges of business development. "It's the perfect tool for developing business," she says. "You may get early wins and think you don't need it, but eventually you will."

> "When you see business development as a marathon—not a sprint—you understand that what you pour in will eventually come back."
>
> **—Milana Hogan**

Grit, as Hogan explains, is a behavioral trait, something within our control and not simply innate. "It's how you are operating. Are you bringing passion and perseverance to your pursuits? Are you choosing to commit to the long game? For women, especially those encountering structural or cultural obstacles in law firms, the ability to push forward through setbacks is critical."

"We used to think intelligence was fixed, but now we know it's not," she adds. "You can train yourself to be smarter, to be more resilient. These are mutable traits. You can dial them up."

The concept of "gritty teams" also emerges in her work. In a 2023 ABA study, Hogan and her collaborators turned their focus from individuals to teams—and discovered that cultivating collective grit and a growth mindset leads to better outcomes, including stronger collaboration and improved retention of women.

"If you're running a team in a gritty, growth-oriented way, mistakes aren't seen as failures but as learning opportunities," Hogan explains. "That kind of environment gives people permission to take the risks that lead to business development. And when people are thriving, they're more likely to stay."

She's quick to point out that firms need to reinforce these traits not just rhetorically but structurally. That includes embedding them into performance evaluations—asking whether lawyers are engaged, persistent, and resilient.

And like others, she believes it means modeling the behavior from the top. "Leaders need to tell their own grit stories. I like to say, 'Let me show you—I emailed them every year on their birthday.

I laid the groundwork.' That takes effort and planning, but that's how relationships grow."

Hogan also advocates for structured training—starting from day one. "If we say marketing is a muscle, then we need to help people build it. That means curriculum. That means storytelling. That means communication skills. You can't just say 'be gritty' and then not offer the support to do it."

As someone who once hesitated to walk into a crowded room and start making connections, Hogan sees grit as empowering—particularly for women who may not see themselves as "natural" rainmakers. "It's not about innate charm. It's about deciding to put in the work, to do the reps. The evidence shows that repetition is the differentiator."

In Hogan's own story, grit has played a defining role. Her dissertation on women in Big Law caught the attention of the ABA, sparking a decade-long project on grit and a growth mindset. She says "yes" to opportunities, even when they don't make perfect sense on paper—because she knows that showing up matters.

"You make your own luck," she says. "When you see business development as a marathon—not a sprint—you understand that what you pour in will eventually come back."

Facing the Odds: Tshepo Shabangu

Tshepo Shabangu grew up in one of South Africa's townships—segregated communities designated as Black-only areas under apartheid. These areas were shaped by systemic exclusion, and residents were barred from living in white neighborhoods. Opportunities were scarce, and outsiders often didn't grasp the depth of the challenges faced by those who lived there.

At age eleven, Tshepo was selected as one of the top ten Black students in her township to participate in an after school special language program. Sponsored by the German government, the initiative allowed her to study German at one of the local German schools. True to her nature—someone who finishes what she starts—she completed all four years of the program, and through many years of practice, became fluent in the language.

After earning her undergraduate degree, Tshepo was invited to study in Germany. But before she could begin, she needed to pass a university-level proficiency exam in German. She did and was admitted. Still, the transition wasn't easy. It was the early 1990s, and in Germany she often felt isolated. Few people looked like her. The sense of displacement was initially overwhelming.

During her first month, Tshepo called her father and told him she wanted to come home. He listened, then gave her the advice that would shape the course of her life. "We want you back," he said, "but knowing you, you'll never forgive yourself if you don't finish what you started. Stay one more month. If you still want to come home after that, you can." She stayed.

Over the following weeks, she demonstrated what Milana Hogan referred to as grit. She began reaching out to others, building community, and finding her footing in a place that initially felt so foreign. Her persistence paid off. She went on to earn her degree in German, obtained magna cum laude and built a powerful foundation for her legal career. It wasn't easy, but her determination, adaptability, and grit saw her through.

Early in her career, she sought out connections by joining local chambers of commerce, law societies, and international associations like the U.S.-based National Bar Association (NBA)—using her own funds to travel abroad, attend NBA Conventions and form relationships with lawyers who shared her background. Her resourcefulness and drive led her to becoming a partner at various law firms and finally making her home in one of Africa's leading IP firms, Spoor & Fisher, where she has practiced for more than two decades.

A polyglot who speaks eight languages, Tshepo views cultural fluency as essential to client development. "I don't know how someone can do business in Africa without understanding all the different nuance," she explained. "That cultural competency is very important for every rainmaker."

She tailors her approach depending on the norms of the client—whether that means knowing when not to make eye contact out of cultural respect or adapting her tone to suit German, Japanese, or African business customs. Her service mindset goes well beyond technical legal work, which she considers "the bare minimum." In one case, she invited a female client to stay in her home, helped her organize an internal filing system for her company, and even hand-delivered an IP book, in which she co-authored a chapter—actions that ultimately contributed to the client rerouting all their global IP work through her firm.

Above all, Tshepo views business development as an opportunity to serve and uplift others. "People help those who have helped them," she said. "I make it about them, not me." That philosophy also shapes how she mentors young women in her firm and the legal profession. She ensures that junior lawyers—especially women—don't just accompany her to client meetings but actively participate. "I never want to go to a client presentation with people who are not going to say anything, and I always ensure that team members contribute." While she admits that she is not comfortable with self-promotion, she's quick to advise the next generation to articulate their accomplishments: "I think the younger lawyers today have to tell people what they've done. I haven't been good at that—but they must be better."

Think Piece

What Can We Learn from Mentors and Other Professionals?

By Sally King*

I've enjoyed a long career in and around the legal profession. I started as the first COO of GE's Legal Department, working with Ben Heinemann in 1990, and remained largely in-house until 2001. By that point, I had moved to NYNEX and worked on the mergers between NYNEX and Bell Atlantic, as well as Bell Atlantic and GTE to form Verizon. Then, a left turn and I stepped over the transom and joined the then-growing but still relatively small ranks of COOs in law firms. I finally retired from COOdom in 2023 and am enjoying my consulting practice. All of this relates because I have enjoyed some excellent mentors as well as some dubious ones.... And I also like to think I have been a good mentor to many.

Hopefully, early on in your career, there were some natural mentors who saw you and recognized your potential and encouraged you gently, and you learned from them. I was fortunate at GE to be surrounded by some super smart and confident people who were

---

* Sally King is a seasoned international executive known for her expertise in global operations, strategic planning, and merger integration within the professional services industry. With more than thirty years of experience, Ms. King has navigated complex challenges and orchestrated transformative initiatives for both law firms and major corporations, consistently driving profitability and productivity enhancements.

Having served in key leadership roles at prestigious organizations such as General Electric, NYNEX, Clifford Chance, and Akin Gump Strauss Hauer & Feld, Ms. King has honed her skills in firm leadership succession planning, merger integration, corporate governance, talent management and operations.

Ms. King's strategic foresight and hands-on approach are key to reshaping organizational structures, driving cultural transformations, and fostering innovation amid dynamic industry landscapes.

empowered to take steps to improve every aspect of GE—including the team around them. I learned so much from Ben's leadership and felt empowered by him to act and do my best work. While much was written at the time (and since) about the culture at GE, I can honestly say that the early 90's at GE were pretty incredible and a culture of excellence and respect prevailed. I was one of the lucky ones, who not only felt I was able to stay and succeed, but also, when a wonderful opportunity fell into my lap, I was celebrated as I left.

Sadly, not every organization provides such a backdrop and not every leader is blessed with the innate ability to mentor. I actually don't believe you can search for a mentor, I believe they fall into your lap—you just have to be open to the idea that not all mentors are senior to you in your organization. Happily, mentors come in all shapes and sizes. Over the years, I have been (perhaps unwittingly for them) mentored by people who reported to me, people who were not employed at the same firm, and frankly even my (now grown) daughters.

One of my first mentors was actually a recruiter. She was an amazing lady, who at the time I was determined to impress. She reached out to me for a job she had been retained to fill, and I was one of the people she presented to the firm. I was ready. And anxious for my next step. I was not the successful candidate and was, I think it fair to say, more than a little upset when I was not selected. Carol not only provided feedback but encouraged me to keep following my dreams. At many turns in my career, Carol was a sounding board—and someone I knew I could count on to be direct and non-judgmental. While she never actually placed me, we became firm friends—and yes, she was an invaluable mentor. Sadly, she died some years ago. Sometimes there is just a connection that makes sense and is too good to pass up. I like to think that I provided solid friendship to Carol too.

Another atypical mentor was a CIO who reported to me. I won't name him—he is still in his role and would be mortified, I think. So let's call him Dave. Dave is an introvert. When we hired him, he took great pains to be super prepared for every (many steps in a law firm) interview. And took the Personality Assessment the recruiter provided. Which clearly demonstrated his analytical and technical comfort levels. I believed that Dave had the technical chops, but I had concerns about his ability to lead a large and critically important team. His recommendations spoke to many strong attributes and we hired him. Dave exceeded all of my expectations and I learned so much from him. Dave insisted that everyone on his team (candidly a team of people that were more comfortable talking to each other and machines) get away from their workspace for at least four hours every week to roam the practice floors and interact with lawyers and staff to find out what the pain points were and how they could help. Yes, it was awkward at first. But I can honestly report that we had the best IT team with the highest level of respect from the lawyers and staff of any firm I have worked with. Dave made sure that he took the time to listen. He wasn't afraid to push back, but he improved the team's offerings and solutions every day. I learned so much by watching his leadership style, and clearly his team loved him.

I say all of this to demonstrate that mentors aren't always who you expect them to be, and sometimes they don't know they are mentors. But they are just the same.

I also hope that everyone reading this is already a mentor (or aspires to be one). I am certain that many of the women in this book have talked about supporting other women. This is particularly important when you are in a position of leadership and perhaps someone who is a rising star is not in the room. It is so important to be the voice "in the room" for those who are not there and to acknowledge the contribution of others rather than take the glory for the efforts of others.

Finally, and sadly, the notion of women not being heard even when they have a seat at the table seems to continue to be a battle. In one organization where I had a seat at the table with, yes, a minority of women (perhaps three or four out of twenty), the women came together and agreed that they would work hard to support each other. So when "Jane" said something and the discussion moved on, and then "John" essentially repeated what "Jane" said as his own, one of the other women would say "thanks so much for endorsing and repeating what Jane just said." Over time it became very powerful and the men in the room acknowledged what was happening and became more aware.

Look for mentors everywhere. And remember, your network is your most valuable asset. People really do love to help. Give yourself a chance and your network too!

Chapter 9

Practice, Practice, Practice and Be Authentic While Doing It

"The door that nobody else will go in at seems always to swing open widely for me."

—Clara Barton

There are no strong statistics on how many times someone needs to hear a lawyer's name before they are hired. I've heard numbers from three to seven. What I am certain of is that with targeted marketing and practice at pitching business, you will see success. The more you do, the easier it gets. You get better each time.

Be the Authentic You

Authenticity is essential in business development. You're far more likely to follow through on activities that feel natural and energizing to you—and less likely to stick with those that feel forced or uncomfortable. When your approach aligns with your personality, it becomes more sustainable. It also builds trust. Clients and prospects can sense when you are being genuine, and that connection makes all the difference.

Susan Eandi is a labor and employment partner at Baker McKenzie and a great client developer. She has an enormous book of business, yet she challenges the traditional idea of networking, saying she doesn't believe in drawing sharp lines between her personal and professional life. Instead of striving for balance, which she says she tried for years and calls a "losing battle where you never feel like you've really succeeded," she advocates for integration.

She connects with people in every area of her life—clients, friends, fellow dog-walkers—without overthinking it or scheduling it rigidly. "I don't love the word networking. I connect. I integrate." She makes spontaneous, thoughtful gestures, like taking a picture that reminds her of a client and texting it with a simple "thinking of you." This everyday approach to connection is both natural and effective, removing pressure and creating more genuine and long-lasting relationships.

Susan lives in the San Francisco Bay Area, and besides excelling at being a lawyer, she has made getting outside a priority, making time to take (sometimes very early) morning walks. One day, Susan mentioned to a client that she was trying to start her days with morning walks, and the client asked to join her. Together, they started daily walks, adding other clients and friends and friends of friends to the group when schedules permit. Walking with clients and friends wherever she finds herself in the world has not only become a habit, but an enduring way to make a memory and to connect. And most of the time, they are not even discussing business.

Donna Wilson at Manatt says that the element of business development that really made it all work—was being herself.

"I once got great advice from a senior partner after I'd been watching how the men operated in court: crisp suits, three points, polished delivery. I thought I had to mimic that to be successful. But this partner pulled me aside and said, 'You have to be yourself.'

And that clicked. I'm a South Jersey, blue-collar kid. I have a different way of connecting with people, and I leaned into that. It was the best advice I ever got. From that moment on, I stopped trying to be someone else and started leading with my own voice. And that's when things really started to take off."

Can You Be Coached?

Business development isn't something you're born knowing how to do—it's something you train for. Even for professionals whose full-time job is sales, it takes discipline and repetition.

For lawyers, who may not think of themselves as "in sales," the learning curve is even steeper, but also manageable with consistent practice.

According to Sam McKenna, "There needs to be dedicated time in your calendar where you do these activities. Even we as sales professionals are weak at this—and this is all we do." She suggests setting aside regular time for activities like writing LinkedIn posts, following up with contacts, or proactively offering referrals.

Sam also reframes "prospecting" in a more approachable way. "Prospecting can be as uncomplicated as identifying target clients who post on LinkedIn—and then engaging with them. That's prospecting. That's putting your name in their world." Her message is clear: If sales experts need to train and maintain the habit, lawyers—who are balancing countless other demands—need to be even more deliberate. Practice builds confidence, and confidence makes it easier to ask for the business.

In some firms, resources for formal training are limited, so individuals take the initiative to hire their own coaches. Other firms invest more intentionally, offering internal coaching or creating cohort-based programs for new partners and senior associates they see as rising leaders. These programs often include structured coaching to help participants build their practices and leadership skills.

Carolyn Sandano is a certified master coach who specializes in helping lawyers with business development and personal growth. As a former Chief Marketing Officer at a number of Am Law 100 firms, she has the experience to truly make a difference for her clients. "Coaching is an art and a science," she noted. "It's about collaboration with someone who can really hear you. The coach's job is to raise your awareness so you can make your own decisions. My clients, the lawyers, always have the answer already—they just haven't unearthed it yet."

She sees particular value in coaching for women in leadership roles. "There are enormous pressures on women in high-level business. A coach can be your secret weapon—someone who supports you unconditionally and gives you the space and grace to think about what you really want." Still, Carolyn is clear about boundaries: "If someone is in real distress, a good coach will know when to suggest they get additional support. Coaching isn't therapy."

Her advice to anyone considering coaching? "Be clear about why you're hiring a coach. What do you hope to happen when you make this investment?" And most importantly, "You should feel like your coach is 1000% on your side. If that doesn't feel true, they're not the right coach for you."

Lauren Krasnow brings a unique perspective as a former Big Law lawyer, recruiter, and now high-level coach to law firm leaders and partners. Her definition of coachability is rooted in self-awareness and emotional readiness, not just skill-building. "Coaching is about helping someone decide if and how they want to change," she says. "It's not just about taking action—it's about being in touch with your emotions so you can take the *right* action." For her, the best clients are thoughtful, open to self-reflection, and, as she puts it, "people who have a sense of self-awareness and are smart."

She emphasizes the importance of having a deeper motivation, whether it's a specific pain point or the desire to level up. "Coaching takes humility. It can be hard." Lauren has a charming, unexpected filter for client fit: laughter. "Are we laughing during the first chemistry call?," she asks. That sense of ease and mutual respect matters in what can be sensitive discussions.

Her coaching is about more than performance—it's about connection, perspective, and finding levity in the process of personal growth.

Marketing Is Muscle

Jeff Klein, a former partner at Weil, Gotshal & Manges, is now a consultant to clients principally in the sports and entertainment industries and Of Counsel at Clarick, Gueron and Reisbaum. As I mentioned in my first book, *Best Practices in Law Firm Business Development and Marketing*, Jeff believes that developing business is like building muscle. It is a talent that one needs to strengthen by using it over and over again. At first, it might be slightly painful to exercise that talent muscle, but over time it gets better, and the muscle gets stronger.

Jenni Dickson, who rose through the ranks at Patterson Belknap to become the firm's Co-Chief Operating Officer, offered a wonderfully relatable and similar metaphor: Business development is like yoga. "If you do it every so often," she said, "it hurts the next day." Her point was simple but powerful—consistency matters.

Whether weight-bearing exercises or yoga classes, for lawyers, it can be easy to let business development slide during busy periods. But if you wait too long to reconnect with contacts or show up in your professional network, it becomes uncomfortable, even awkward, to restart.

"You don't need to be flashy or constantly selling; you just need to be present. That steady presence—showing up authentically and offering help when it's needed—builds trust over time."

—Jenni Dickson

Jenni emphasized that regular, even small, efforts—like reaching out, sharing an article, or attending an event—help keep the muscles warm. She also described business development as being like a "blinking light" in someone's life. "You don't need to be flashy or constantly selling; you just need to be present. That steady presence—showing up authentically and offering help when it's needed—builds trust over time." This is especially true for litigators, where the client may not always have a new case for which they are seeking counsel.

Jenni notes that staying in a "helping mindset" makes it easier and more natural to maintain connections. Whether it's sending a quick note or checking in without an agenda, being a consistent, low-pressure presence and trusted advisor can be a powerful way to build business without it feeling transactional.

"The skill of getting out and speaking with people, learning about them and their businesses and then being able to either ask for the business or ensure that you're there at the right time to be called, is a craft. It's also a habit you build over time, so it's never too early to start," says Jenni.

Brenda Sharton is the Managing Partner of Dechert's Boston office and is the global Chair of the firm's top-ranked Cyber, Privacy and AI Practice. She echoes the idea. "The more senior I've gotten, the more I've leaned into that—sharing your human side, sharing your personal life. You really bond with clients that way."

How did Brenda start doing that? "It's all about relationships," she says. "I had that advice early—it was to focus on other junior people, stay in touch with your classmates. You don't want to notice that they've just been made a general counsel and have your first contact be, 'Hey, remember me? How about giving me some business?'" And yet, Brenda also believes that having the expertise is a must. "The baseline is excellent work and being super responsive. I've been hyper-responsive my entire career, and I aim to be good about remaining in touch."

Avoiding Perfectionism

Authenticity takes time to gel for many women. Too often, there's an unspoken assumption that women are simply 'better' at organizing things, and as a result, they take on tasks that consume valuable time—time that could be spent developing business or deepening client relationships.

One of the most powerful insights came from my conversation with Jen Leonard, founder of Creative Lawyers and former head of innovation at Penn Carey Law School at The University of Pennsylvania. Jen identifies a tension between perfectionism and business development.

> "[Business development] is a completely different muscle that requires resilience, and we don't have resilience when we're perfectionists."
>
> **—Jen Leonard**

As she explained, many women lawyers are conditioned from an early age to excel in environments where the expectations are clear. The rules are structured, and success is measured by performance, whether in academics or early legal careers. But business development operates in a vastly different terrain.

Jen says, "It's not a game where you're going to be perfect every time. You're going to have to take a hundred swings, and only a few of them are going to work out." For women who have always been rewarded for getting it right the first time, this unpredictability can feel especially daunting.

The implication is profound: To succeed in business development, women must often unlearn the very mindset that helped them thrive in school and at the start of their careers. Jen pointed out that this discomfort with imperfection isn't just about performance—it's also about identity.

When you're used to being seen as competent and in control, putting yourself in a situation where rejection is likely can feel threatening. Jen's insight connects directly to broader themes of resilience, experimentation, and the courage to fail—skills that are just as essential to rainmaking as legal acumen.

As Jen noted, "It's a completely different muscle that requires resilience, and we don't have resilience when we're perfectionists."

Elena's Story: Finding Your Own Voice

Elena Antonetti's story is one of authenticity, connection, and quiet power. Born in Ukraine and now serving as Executive Counsel at Travelers, she brings a thoughtful, international perspective to what it means to be a trusted advisor—and what it takes to build lasting professional relationships. Her background gives her a unique lens. Having grown up outside the United States, Elena is acutely aware of how it feels to walk into a room where you're different, where you're learning as you go. That awareness has shaped how she connects with people, including outside counsel.

She's not looking solely for technical knowledge and "academic perfection" when hiring a lawyer from the outside, she's also looking for counsel who demonstrates authenticity, consistency, and empathy. "Meaningful legal support is not limited to being professional and knowledgeable," she told me. "It's about putting in the time, making your client feel valued, and building trust, that ensures that your connection will last."

Elena believes that small gestures go a long way. The lawyers who stand out in her memory aren't the ones who sent the fanciest pitch or the lengthiest bio listing their achievements. They're the ones who would come through for her when she was in-house counsel working through a challenging issue, while making their clients feel good about the process. They were the ones that empathized with the complexity of the matter and said: "That's a very interesting question you are raising" or "This is an unsettled area, but you're really ahead of the game and on the right track." Those seemingly small comments can make a big difference in someone's day and go a long way in de-escalating the crisis mode, especially when they come in a high-pressure moment. "At any level, we all need to hear that someone whose judgment we trust has our back and that we're doing a remarkable job," she said.

One of the meaningful professional relationships she developed was with Rebecca Eisner, a former managing partner at Mayer Brown. When Elena was a junior Corporate Counsel at Pepsi Bottling Group, Rebecca flew in to introduce herself and share how her team could support Elena's legal needs. At the time, Rebecca was working part-time while raising young kids—a detail she shared honestly when Elena asked about it. Elena recalls that Rebecca exemplified grace and knowledge but was not shying away from acknowledging the challenge of being a working mom. "No one had ever asked me what it was like," Rebecca told her. That professional yet authentic connection stayed with Elena. When Elena later moved to Travelers, she reached out to Rebecca again—not because of a formal pitch, but because of the trust built over time.

"Despite being extraordinarily busy and professionally successful, Rebecca went the extra mile to make people feel seen," Elena said. "To me, that's a sign of outstanding counsel."

When I asked Elena what advice she'd give to younger women trying to build their network, she didn't hesitate: Be true to yourself. "I really dislike when people tell women that being aggressive is 'a must' to succeed," she said. Instead, she urges young lawyers to think about who they are, what they enjoy, and to approach networking in a way that feels natural to them. "If you hate public speaking, don't force it; it's not the only way to get noticed and expand your network. Find another way to contribute: comment on a LinkedIn post, offer to review or edit an article, connect with a mentor, etc."

At the Association of Corporate Counsel, where Elena has taken on leadership roles including chairing the Real Estate Network and now the Network Leadership Council, she has championed the idea of women lifting each other up. Her story started with joining a 7 a.m. leadership breakfast with other women in-house counsel and turned it into a multi-year journey of community, building personal and professional global networks, and growth.

Elena has grown into the role of a leader. "I used to look at the stage where my peers where presenting or receiving awards and think, 'How did they get there? How do these people know everyone?'" she said. "Now I'm up there as well." It turns out, the path to the stage isn't necessarily about being the loudest voice in the room. It could come from being the most genuine one. Elena also coaches other women how to reach for leadership roles and create and maintain meaningful connections. "A happy life is not tied to your title. Ultimately, prioritizing your own needs and growth in a way that is authentic to you is more important. Declining some opportunities that will take away from your personal balance and wellness might just be the best thing for your longevity in the profession as someone who stays ahead of a burnout," says Elena.

Dale's Story: Bridging Business with Your Talent

Dale Cendali, a partner at Kirkland & Ellis, is one of the most influential intellectual property litigators in the country, widely known for building a distinguished career that merges her deep love of the arts with the practice of law. Encouraged early on by her mother, a talented English teacher who wished she could have been a lawyer herself, Dale followed her academic passions to Yale University, where she graduated Phi Beta Kappa and summa cum laude with a degree in history. She was also president of the Yale Dramatic Association, a role that hinted at her future talent for producing, organizing, and managing complex projects—skills that later served her well in the courtroom. Combining her love of reading, writing, and arguing, she attended Harvard Law School, determined to find a way to unite her interests in storytelling and culture with legal practice.

After law school, Dale began her career in general litigation but was always drawn to the then-underappreciated field of intellectual property. At a time when few big firms emphasized IP, she carved out a niche for herself by writing scholarly articles, joining bar groups, and becoming known within her firm for her expertise. One early turning point came when she successfully defended the broadcast of O.J. Simpson's wedding video, during the time of his high-profile criminal case.

From there, Dale's career blossomed, leading to high-stakes work for Warner Bros. and the landmark Harry Potter series, including the pivotal fair use case against the Harry Potter lexicon. Her strategic thinking and courtroom skill eventually earned her two arguments before the U.S. Supreme Court and many appellate wins for clients such as Fox, Astronics and Pepsi.

In 2009, Dale joined Kirkland & Ellis, where she founded and now leads a world-class group with a broad scope and experience in the technology, entertainment and consumer product industries.

She built a diverse, top-tier team with a reputation for excellence and inclusion. Dale recruited a number of team members from the class she teaches at Harvard Law School on copyright and trademark litigation.

Not only is she highly ranked by many legal publications, as both as an IP expert and trial lawyer, she is a passionate supporter of the arts. Dale serves on the boards of the American Theatre Wing (where she is a Tony voter), Harvard's A.R.T., and the Comic Book Legal Defense Fund. She continues to mentor young lawyers, champion authenticity in client development, and finds joy in integrating her personal passions with professional success.

Her practice is not only shaped by technical expertise, but also by a commitment to staying ahead of legal trends and cultivating meaningful relationships throughout her career. Dale is a strong advocate for building a career—and a client base—rooted in authenticity. She emphasizes that marketing should never feel like an act, but rather an extension of who you genuinely are. "You have to have something to sell," she says, "and then let people know you have it." But she also cautions against feeling pressure to adopt every popular tactic. "I rarely use social media professionally," she admits. "I tend to use a more personal approach."

Instead, she focuses on showing clients her expertise through speeches, CLE presentations and of course victories in relevant cases, yet she also likes to combine client development with her own interests. "Taking clients to the theater, is something I love." It's also something Dale knows well as a Tony voter and board member of the American Theatre Wing. "I have a free ticket anyway," she jokes, "so I'll say, 'I'm going. Want to come?'" For Dale, the key is simple: "Do the marketing that's authentic to you." She encourages young lawyers, especially women, to think about their personal brand and business development from the very start—not as something to take up "eventually when you make partner," but from day one.

"Think about it from the perspective of who's hiring you—why you?" she asks. "Do you have great expertise? Are you super responsive? Are you industry-savvy? What makes you stand out?" Dale's advice is to develop real substance and let your strengths be known, not just through your work but also through things like bar involvement, articles, and speaking.

"Think about it from the perspective of who's hiring you—why you?"

—Dale Cendali

"You could be the world's best lawyer, but if you're just manifesting that in your private office, no one will know." To avoid the discomfort of self-promotion, she recommends a thoughtful workaround: "It's easier to toot someone else's horn than to toot your own." She and her peers began the practice of celebrating each other's wins—like writing an article or landing a committee role—and sharing it with others, helping each other gain visibility.

And in client pitches, she notes, "It's a lot easier for a colleague to say, 'Dale teaches at Harvard,' or 'Dale just won this case,' than for me to say it myself." Her message is clear. Success doesn't come from pretending to be someone else. It comes from knowing who you are, what you care about, and finding ways to share that with the world.

Hanim Hamzah's Story: Building a Global Practice with Purpose and Partnership

Hanim Hamzah's trajectory—from a young associate in Malaysia to managing partner of ZICO, then as Asia-Pacific leader at a global KPMG, and today as a partner at King & Wood Mallesons, based in Beijing—is a testament to how clarity, collaboration, and courage can create opportunity.

She described her leadership style as empowering rather than controlling. "You have to set parameters and be clear on what you won't compromise. But beyond that, you give people room to lead their own practices. You're not micromanaging—these are smart people! If you listen, if you're humble, and if you support others the way you were supported, that's where the real leadership happens."

Internally, one of the biggest obstacles I've observed is the difficulty many women have in saying no. Women are frequently asked to take on administrative tasks, organize meetings, lead events, or represent the firm at various functions. While these responsibilities may be valuable, they don't always contribute to the growth of their practice.

Hanim's career is a testament to what's possible when passion, courage, and mentorship come together. As the Asia-Pacific Regional Leader of Legal Services at KPMG, she practiced law and built teams across five jurisdictions—the United Kingdom, Japan, Malaysia, Indonesia, and Singapore. Along the way, she has navigated vastly different cultural norms, gender expectations, and approaches to business development, all while staying grounded in her values and evolving as both a lawyer and a leader.

Her experience in Tokyo revealed the constraints of a rigid corporate culture where drinking late into the night was a business expectation, and support for working mothers was minimal. In contrast, Singapore's more balanced and inclusive environment has allowed Hanim—and many of her female peers—to thrive.

With more women in senior in-house roles and greater access to affordable help at home, the professional playing field feels a bit more level to Hanim. Even the way relationships are built has changed. "In Singapore, business development can happen over lunch, yoga, or a book club," she noted. "It's about finding what works for you and your client." Now a mother herself, Hanim speaks with deep empathy about the challenges facing young women lawyers who are trying to balance home, clients, and self-expectation. "It's hard," she said. "There's a real tension, and sometimes you feel like you're disappointing yourself." Her honesty underscores the pressure many women experience in silence.

One of the most pivotal moments in Hanim's career came when her chair took the time to actively sponsor her. He brought her to meetings, introduced her to clients, and gave her speaking opportunities. That exposure changed everything. "It takes time, and it takes practice," she said. "You don't become good at business development overnight." She believes law firms must be more intentional—offering training, structured development programs, and clear paths for sponsorship. She also noted that while many senior men have been generous with their support, women don't always sponsor each other in the same way. "Some feel they got there on their own, so you should too—but we need to change that."

"Find your passion and then find your team.
You don't work alone—you succeed when you
collaborate, mentor, and grow together."

—Hanim Hamzah

Hanim's story also illustrates the importance of self-awareness and values. She encourages younger lawyers to be clear about their boundaries and guiding principles. In her view, building a business isn't just about technical skill—it's about empathy, collaboration, and integrity. She summed it up beautifully: "Find your passion and then find your team. You don't work alone—you succeed when you collaborate, mentor, and grow together."

Think Piece

What Got You Here Won't Get You There: Permission to Ditch Perfectionism and Start Doing It Your Way

By Jordana Confino*

"What got you here won't get you there."

This is the hard truth that prompted me—and many of the women lawyers I work with—to finally open ourselves to the possibility of rethinking our perfectionism.

But first, let me back up and introduce myself.

My name is Jordana, and I'm a recovering lawyer and Type A+ perfectionist.

Like so many in the legal profession, I wore my perfectionism as a badge of honor for years, convinced it was the secret to my success.

My raging sense of imposter syndrome had me certain that I was neither smarter nor more talented than anyone in the room. But my willingness to dig deeper, work harder, and contort myself to please, perfect, and perform? *That*, I believed, set me apart.

And for a while, it did.

Until it didn't.

---

* Jordana Confino is an attorney, certified professional coach, and founder of JC Coaching & Consulting, a company devoted to helping perfectionists get out of their own way and empowering lawyers to enjoy greater satisfaction and sustainable success in their lives and work. She is also an adjunct professor at Fordham Law School, where she previously served as the Assistant Dean of Professionalism. In her blog, Chronicles of a Recovering Type A+ Perfectionist, Jordana shares stories and offers science-backed tips and strategies for reining in fear and cultivating joy, love, and values-based living in the legal profession.

Eventually, I learned the hard way that my perfectionism was no longer propelling me forward. Quite the contrary—it had started holding me back.

I am not alone in this.

Many of my clients have come to realize that the perfectionist approach they took to being a standout associate worker bee is not going to cut it as they strive to level up, step into their power, and assume the higher-level responsibilities of their new roles—chief among them business development.

This work requires not just diligence, but also creativity, authenticity, and risk tolerance—all of which perfectionism tends to stifle.

To be clear: I'm *not* suggesting that you abandon your drive, attention to detail, or commitment to excellence. You still need all of those to excel.

But perfectionism is distinct from all of those positive attributes. At its core, it's nothing more than a fear and shame-based hustle to prove your worth.

To quote Elizabeth Gilbert:

> "[P]erfectionism is just fear in fancy shoes and a mink coat, pretending to be elegant when actually it's just terrified. Because underneath that shiny veneer, perfectionism is nothing more than a deep existential angst that says, again and again, 'I am not good enough and I will never be good enough.'"[1]

And that angst, if left unchecked, is incompatible with building a sustainable book of business.

Why?

Because when you're operating from a fear-based mindset, you're susceptible to:

---

1. Elizabeth Gilbert, Big Magic: Creative Living Beyond Fear (Penguin Publishing Group 2015).

- **Perfectionist paralysis:** You don't share your ideas unless they're "just right"—which often means you don't share them at all. (Confession: I nearly turned down the opportunity to write this very piece because I feared I'd lack the time to perfect it. *That's* the voice of perfectionism, convincing us that if we can't do something flawlessly, we shouldn't do it at all.)
- **Overextension:** You're a fervent people-pleaser and struggle to set boundaries, especially around billable work. You feel you must constantly say yes to everything, deliver at 110%, and never disappoint. But if you're devoting all your time and energy to busting billables, you'll never have space to nurture the relationships that are equally essential for your success.
- **Lack of authenticity:** You've mastered the art of emulating what you deem to be the cookie-cutter rainmaker ideal—polished, persuasive, and always on. But you're not showing up as yourself. And unlike other aspects of lawyering, business development is a human sport: The most powerful client relationships are built on trust and genuine connection, not performance.

While these tendencies are typically deeply ingrained, the good news is they're not intractable.

Tools like self-compassion, growth mindset, and values alignment can help us loosen their grip and empower us to finally start playing to win, as opposed to merely playing not to lose.

And it's well worth the effort to cultivate these tools, because what I've seen—time and again—is that the women who thrive in business development are the ones who are willing to replace perfectionism with a more authentic, vulnerable approach.

They stop treating business development like a performance—or some sort of test they need to pass.

They stop overpreparing and underestimating themselves.

Instead, they start showing up as their true selves—with courage, conviction, compassion, and care.

They speak on panels even when their inner critic whispers someone else would be better.

They hit publish on articles (or book segments!) even when that same voice objects.

They reach out to people they genuinely respect and then listen and respond—rather than reciting from a premade script.

They lead with their values, share their real stories, offer unique perspectives, and trust that they deserve business (heck, they're freaking dynamite!) just as they are.

And they do it consistently—even (especially) when it sets them apart.

Because at the end of the day, enduring clients are drawn to people—not polish—and it's authenticity, empathy, loyalty, and reliability—not perfection—that build lasting trust.

So if you've been waiting to start your business development efforts until you feel more credentialed, "ready," or perfect, please consider this your permission slip (and gentle nudge of encouragement) to begin now—authentically, and on your own terms.

There may be no one "right" way to build a book of business.

But the *wrong* way is by trying to be someone you're not.

You already have everything you need—you just need to stop editing it out.

Chapter 10

How Law Firms Can Help Women Lawyers Develop Business

"Learning is not attained by chance; it must be sought for with ardor and diligence."

—Abigail Adams

There is a great deal that law firms can do to support both men and women as they progress in their careers. Business development training, appropriate technology and intentional programing should be a major part of that effort.

Training, at all stages of one's career, is a necessity. Some of the arguments against such training are, frankly, shortsighted.

One common objection is: *"If we train our associates, they'll take that talent elsewhere."* Of course, associates may eventually leave. But if they do, they're likely to leave with a better feeling about your firm—if they are grateful for the investment you made in them. Providing training on how to build relationships and develop a practice is a meaningful gesture that, in many cases, doesn't cost the firm very much. And if your training is part of a broader strategy that includes ongoing development and opportunities for advancement, it's far more likely that your associates will choose to stay.

Another myth: *"Training is too expensive."* Not necessarily. Yes, you can bring in high-level consultants or coaches to create tailored programs—especially useful if your internal teams are already at capacity. But training doesn't always have to be elaborate. It can be as simple as organizing a regularly scheduled panel of successful rainmakers to speak with associates about how they built their books of business. Or it might be a session with your business development team, explaining the resources available to help associates maintain and build connections.

And then there's the third myth: *"Associates should be busy being associates. We already have rainmaking partners to do this work for the rest of the firm."* This isn't just a myth—it's a warning sign. Firms that don't think long term about generational growth and fail to train their next generation of business developers may not be around in the decades to come. Relying solely on today's rainmakers without building a pipeline for tomorrow is a strategy with a short shelf life.

You can also invest in enterprise tools—like a user-friendly CRM system or LinkedIn enablement tools—that make marketing and business development more accessible and efficient. These tools can provide structure and scale and further professionalize informal or ad hoc efforts.

Training should also be responsive to where a lawyer is in their career. For junior associates, the focus should be on relationship-building: staying in touch with law school classmates, making connections through external experiences, and understanding the basics of networking. As lawyers advance, more targeted training becomes helpful—how to nurture potential clients, how to make introductions within the firm, and how to ask for business.

Too often, firms assume that once an associate makes partner, they're fully formed. The same is true for laterals—firms may assume they come in with everything they need. But many of these lawyers still need support: coaching, business development guidance, or simply a better understanding of the firm's capabilities and how to leverage them.

"You can't leave it to chance," Hanim Hamzah said of law firm business development. "Some partners are really good at the work—but that doesn't mean they know how to build a book of business. They may not have the confidence, or they just haven't had the exposure." She emphasized that formal training and mentorship are essential: "When I was transitioning into leadership, my chair took me to meetings and conferences all over the world. He gave me the chance to speak, introduced me to key people, and pushed me outside my comfort zone. It was that visibility and practice that made the difference." She believes law firms should offer structured programs: "It's not enough to say, 'go network.' People need exposure, coaching, and real opportunities," says Hanim.

The bottom line: All lawyer training—including business development training—shouldn't be viewed as a one-time event. It should be continuous and woven into a lawyer's journey at the firm—from associate to making partner and beyond.

Business Development Can Be Taught

Lise Lotte Hjerrild of Horten is clear on the talent needed to develop business. Lise Lotte says, "Business development isn't an inborn talent—it's a teachable skill."

In the early years of her career, Lise Lotte devoted herself entirely to legal work. "I spent a lot of time focused on my assignments and assumed that was enough," she says. "I wasn't great at developing business—I hadn't been taught how."

> "Business development isn't an inborn talent—it's a teachable skill."
>
> **—Lise Lotte Hjerrild**

That changed when she was recruited by a forward-thinking firm that lacked a corporate M&A group but made a strategic investment in business development. "They had a CMO and we used an external coach, and they rocked my world," she recalls. "They showed me how business development wasn't just something other people did—it was something I could learn, systematize, and build into my practice."

Today, Lise Lotte is a firm believer in training lawyers at all levels. "Training can make people better at business development," she explains. "It's not just about hiring new people. With the right guidance, anyone can improve and contribute to the firm's success."

Lynda Bennett, chair of Lowenstein Sandler's Insurance Recovery Group and co-founder and leader of the firm's Women's Initiative Network, has spent nearly a decade shaping that employee resource group. What began as informal cocktail hours evolved into a strategic, intentional organization that is focused on creating connection, candid conversation, and community across all practice areas and levels of seniority within the firm. "We realized that women needed a safe space to talk about things that don't always get discussed—microaggressions, pregnancy complications, the real business of law, mental health, how to navigate maternity leave, and bringing your game face to work while facing personal challenges," Lynda shared. "We built a structure that allows for real talk—and that has built real trust." Now celebrating its tenth anniversary, Lowenstein's Women's Initiative Network has become a foundational part of the firm's culture, with programming that ranges from intimate roundtables to firmwide panels featuring junior associates sharing their career journeys. It also serves as a core recruitment and retention tool for top talent.

"People often think networking means walking into a big room full of strangers and leaving with new work. But we reframed it. Networking is about staying connected to people you already know, like your accountant, friends in your kids' play groups, or even a former classmate."

—Lynda Bennett

One of their earliest and most successful programs focused on helping mid-level (fourth to sixth year) associates—which included but was not limited to women—learn how to build relationships and generate business in a way that felt accessible. "People often think networking means walking into a big room full of strangers and leaving with new work. But we reframed it. Networking is about staying connected to people you already know, like your accountant, friends in your kids' play groups, or even a former classmate."

Lynda explains, "It really is about giving, giving, and then maybe getting." Participants were assigned monthly "homework"—three external and three internal meetings—and then regrouped to discuss what worked and what didn't. "We broke it down, we de-fanged the process," Lynda said. Lesley added, "That is partially how I built my accountant network. I started meeting people not to pitch, but to discuss new tax rules and regulations—and those turned into referrals."

Mary Wilson shared several innovative initiatives from Dentons. One is *Excel*, a 360-degree mentorship program that pairs leaders at the firm with junior and mid-level associates. Another is a *Mock Pitch Competition*, where seventy-five associates responded to an RFP and pitched to firm leadership—gaining exposure, feedback, and real-world business development skills. Dentons also runs *Preparing for Rain*, a program targeting associates at the five-year mark to build client development. "These initiatives are designed not only to develop skills, but to build visibility and confidence across our talent pool," she said.

Early Exposure

Ingrid Pierce at Walkers is passionate about preparing associates for long-term success—not just as lawyers, but as future business generators. At Walkers, she's helped implement training and support systems to ensure that associates start thinking about client development from the outset. "The worst thing is when someone becomes partner and says, 'I don't know anyone . . . I've just been sitting in my office for eight years.'"

She sees this as a fixable problem—one that stems from a lack of early exposure and guidance, not a lack of potential. That's why Walkers encourages participation in legal associations and networks, industry committees, and even tailored business development coaching before a lawyer heads out on a trip or joins a pitch.

"The idea is not to overwhelm them, but to give them the tools," Ingrid explains. "If you haven't had that first exposure—that first trip, that first panel, that first conversation—it can be intimidating. We give them a framework and then help them build confidence from there."

Her approach to business development training blends realism with optimism. Ingrid knows not everyone will have the same style or comfort level with networking, but she believes strongly that with exposure, guidance, and opportunity, every associate can find their voice and start developing relationships long before they're expected to bring in business. It's not about turning young lawyers into extroverts—it's about giving them the chance to build meaningful connections early, while they're still forming their professional identity.

Elevating Talent at All Career Stages

When Jami McKeon became Chair of Morgan Lewis—the first woman to hold that position in the firm's more than 150-year history—she brought with her not only deep litigation expertise but also a sharp eye for how to develop and elevate talent. One of her signature initiatives is ML Women, a program she launched with a clear and deliberate focus: to support business development across the firm by amplifying the strength and impact of its women partners.

"We've got these amazing women . . . unlike most firms, we have more than 30% women in our partnership, and we have some of the best and brightest," she said. "Clients want access to outstanding women lawyers. Sometimes they want a different perspective. Sometimes it matters that their lawyers look like their own teams. Whatever the reason, we need to harness that talent—not only for their benefit but for the benefit of all our clients."

Importantly, ML Women is not positioned as a traditional networking or affinity group. Jami was determined to break that mold. As she put it, "ML Women is 100% a business development focus and 0% a networking focus."The program isn't about creating a separate lane for women; it's about expanding opportunity for everyone at the firm by showcasing its strengths to clients. "It's not about choosing one person over another. It's about how can we help all of our partners, including our male partners, by giving clients access to that talent," she added.

ML Women exemplifies how inclusive initiatives can be strategically aligned with client service and firm growth. By grounding the program in the firm's core mission—delivering excellent legal work to clients—and by treating business development as a shared enterprise, Jami has not only elevated the role of women at Morgan Lewis but redefined what it means to lead with intention.

"It's not about choosing one person over another. It's about how we can help all of our partners, including our male partners, by giving clients access to that talent."

—Jami McKeon

Ellen Kaye Fleishhacker is the Global Co-Chair of Arnold & Porter and a leader in the firm's investment management group. Ellen feels strongly that training shouldn't stop once you become a partner.

The firm recognized during the pandemic that they needed to enhance the ways that they prepare recently promoted partners and counsel—men and women—to continue their professional growth and to become business developers. As a result, they created the Arnold & Porter Executive Leadership Academy—"APEX"—which provides training, coaching, mentoring, and networking opportunities to support and advance their professional and business development efforts.

"To build a thriving practice, it is essential to have a strong internal support cohort, in addition to your client network. APEX provides that vital space for fostering collaboration, strengthening leadership skills, and sustaining long-term career growth." Ellen said. The program is a two-year curriculum that leverages both internal and external resources, such as speakers, individual and group coaching, and periodic meetings for each participant with the firm's Chief Business Development & Marketing Officer and

Business Development teams. The program also includes mentoring and networking components.

APEX creates a forum for participants to share their business development challenges, including (but not limited by) those faced by women, and to talk about strategies to overcome them. The various types of settings, from group to individual coaching to mentoring, provide each person with whatever venue they feel is most valuable to raise those concerns and help work through them. This flexibility allows each participant to engage in ways that feel authentic and empowering to them. The program also builds a strong sense of community, reinforcing that lawyers are not alone in their experiences, can learn from each other, and can support each other in achieving long-term success.

Inside Two Signature Programs at Blake, Cassels & Graydon LLP

One of the most enduring challenges in the legal profession is not just how to support women in their roles today, but how to prepare them for what comes next—whether that's a seat in the C-suite or a place at the boardroom table. Few firms have taken on that challenge as systematically and successfully as Blake, Cassels & Graydon LLP, one of Canada's top business law firms.

Alison Jeffrey, Senior Advisor, Strategic Initiatives and Client Development Coach at Blakes, also leads the firm's women's program. Blakes has several programs in place to support the advancement of women in law and business. One of those programs is focused on advancing women GCs on boards. By doing so, Blakes is shining a light on a talented pipeline of board candidates, expanding leadership opportunities in the boardroom and building strong relationships cemented in client growth and success.

Alison's passion for supporting women in leadership began at an early age. She was inspired by her mother and father. While there were no role models for her mother to follow back then, she set her aspirations on becoming involved in local government and eventually serving as one of the first women mayors of a Canadian city. Her ally and champion in this pursuit was Alison's father. "They were a dynamic duo!" says Alison. As she grew up, Alison watched and learned from this partnership. "My mother worked hard and exceled at everything she did, and my father worked equally hard as my mother's campaign manager." Their collective efforts were rewarded when Alison's mother ran for mayor and won.

Blakes offers its women lawyers two signature programs—*Stepping Up: Preparing to Be a General Counsel* and *Women GCs on Boards*.

Launched in 2014, *Stepping Up* is one of the longest-running and most celebrated initiatives of its kind for women in-house counsel in Canada. The program recently celebrated its ten-year anniversary—a milestone not only in longevity but in impact. Its focus is simple but ambitious: to increase the number of women General Counsel across Canadian public and private companies, not-for-profits, government agencies, and Canadian subsidiaries of multinationals.

While many programs in the legal world offer generic leadership training, *Stepping Up* is unapologetically skills-focused. "It's designed to provide practical, real-world guidance on how to move from a senior in-house counsel role into the GC seat. It's not about theory—it's about readiness." says Alison.

What makes the program especially compelling is its track record. Year after year, it has helped elevate talented women lawyers into broader leadership roles, all while fostering confidence, business acumen, and an understanding of the pressures that come with being a General Counsel in today's evolving business environment.

If *Stepping Up* helps women reach the top of the legal department, *Women GCs on Boards* is about what happens next—recognizing and preparing women General Counsels as prime candidates for board service.

The idea for the program was sparked during a candid conversation between the firm's chairman and the Chief Legal Officer of a major Canadian bank. She voiced a frustration that many had quietly shared: despite their deep expertise and strategic insight, General Counsels—especially women—were rarely seen as viable board candidates. It wasn't about ability. It was about visibility.

This insight became a catalyst. The firm's marketing and research teams got to work, analyzing 2016 data from the S&P/TSX Composite Index to determine how many boards included General Counsels, and whether those roles were held by men or women, active GCs or retired ones. The data painted a clear picture: GCs were underrepresented on boards, but it also revealed a good news story—women GCs exceeded gender parity with their male counterparts.

But Blakes didn't stop at data. It turned insight into action. In 2017, the *Women GCs on Boards* program was born—and it has been gaining momentum ever since.

What sets these programs apart are three essential elements:

Peer-Led, Experience-Rich Learning. The faculty is made up entirely of sitting General Counsels—both women and men—who share their own journeys, lessons learned, and insider knowledge. Through fireside chats and small-group discussions, participants hear firsthand what it takes to step up to the role of GC and to be board-ready. There are no canned lectures or generic takeaways—just real stories and honest advice.

Nomination-Only Participation. In *Stepping Up*, entry into the program is by nomination, typically from a participant's own GC or direct report. That nomination isn't just an application—it's a vote of confidence. It tells the participant: *You have what it takes—and we see it.* That kind of recognition can be a powerful motivator, and the built-in support from firm leadership adds real weight.

A Built-In Community of Support. Perhaps most striking is the lasting sense of community both programs create. Participants form genuine relationships that continue long after the program ends. Many alumni stay connected and eventually return—not just as mentors and faculty, but as nominators for the next generation. "It's this wonderful cycle—almost like the circle of life," Alison said. And she's right. What's emerging isn't just a talent pipeline. It's a community of women leaders lifting each other up.

Both programs speak to something larger: the value of listening closely to clients and responding with creativity, data, and care. They were born not in a boardroom or a branding session, but in conversations—with clients, with colleagues, with women wondering how to take the next step in their careers.

And that's what makes them so powerful. They're not just programs. They're pathways.

Reinforcing the Right Behaviors and Setting Clear Expectations

A CMO of a top-tier NY-based law firm emphasized the importance of setting clear expectations for business development—even at the associate level. She notes that while motivations and compensation structures vary from firm to firm, the underlying challenges around client development are strikingly consistent. "You have a unique opportunity with young partners and associates to actually be much clearer about the expectations," she explained, whether that means setting hour-based targets or simply encouraging specific behaviors like sharing the firm's content on social media.

"Without intentional steps, firms risk perpetuating an uneven playing field—where leadership and growth opportunities remain siloed and inaccessible to those who haven't yet been 'tapped.'"

—AmLaw 50 CMO

Several firms now circulate a weekly email summarizing recent LinkedIn activity and ask lawyers to engage by liking or sharing one of the featured posts. Setting small expectations is a simple and practical way to start.

Many of the CMOs with whom I spoke believe in empowering women—and all junior partners—with leadership roles that focus squarely on business development. Too often, they observed, women are placed in talent or diversity-related leadership tracks, rather than the business-facing roles, such as leading client teams. One CMO stated, "It's really important to have women in business-focused, client development-focused leadership roles."

Giving someone the opportunity to lead a client team, serve as a deputy lead, or take charge of a major firm event or alumni initiative can provide hands-on exposure to what client development actually looks like in practice. These are the roles where people build confidence, learn how to win business, and gain visibility with both colleagues and clients.

One CMO said, "Without intentional steps, firms risk perpetuating an uneven playing field—where leadership and growth opportunities remain siloed and inaccessible to those who haven't yet been 'tapped.'"

Having the Infrastructure and Technology Tools in Place

Sarah Heaton Concannon, a highly regarded partner at Quinn Emanuel Urquhart & Sullivan LLP, offers a clear-eyed view of what law firms can do to genuinely support business development—and it starts with removing internal roadblocks. "You can't always move fast enough," she says of the conflicts system in place at many firms, particularly when urgent matters like SEC or governmental investigations arise. "Cases come in, and the prospective client needs someone to call the government that day—they can't wait for fifty approvals." She urges firms to be more flexible with conflicts, retainers, and billing structures, especially when the matter comes from a personal contact. "If I get a case that's referred to me by my college roommate, it's far more likely to be something relatively small," she explains, "but by rewarding attorneys starting to build a practice and showing them that, yes, in fact, you can open that case—even if it doesn't meet the firm's usual parameters—you build confidence."

Sarah also points to a disconnect between what some firms say and what they do. "Firms say everyone should be generating work—but then some create systems that only a small group of people can actually navigate," she notes. She calls for less bureaucracy, clearer infrastructure, and more trust in the judgment of their lawyers. Her experience at a prior firm, where coaches and programs were plentiful, left her unconvinced that formal marketing training alone makes a difference. "There were coaches, weekly business development-focused meetings, and a big marketing department, but it didn't seem particularly effective in helping individual attorneys figure out how to get clients." In Sarah's view, firms should focus less on abstract programming and more on making the act of opening and working a case easier—especially for those just beginning to build a book of business.

There are available technologies to support business development that firms can use on an enterprise or firm wide basis.

A customer relationship management system (CRM) especially one tailored specifically for professional services, allows firms to track contact information of clients, prospects and alumni, and much more. By integrating these systems with a lawyer's workflow, it becomes easier for a lawyer to track relationships, identify opportunities and manage pursuits and provides a structure for developing business. A number of these products, including Salesforce, Foundation, Nexl and Dealcloud, have been game changers for law firms.

Laura Saklad understands marketing from both the law firm side and the provider side. For many years, Laura was the Chief Operations Officer at the global law firm Orrick and worked on all forms of strategic matters including growth and business development. Laura is now Vice President, Legal Industry, at Intapp, where she works with law firms to maximize the value derived from the company's products, like Dealcloud, a system that empowers lawyers with data, insight and automation. The system also suggests ideas for discrete actions partners can take to strengthen client relationships and capture opportunities.

Dealcloud captures contact data, past matters, and pitch history, giving marketing and business development teams a comprehensive view of client interactions. This relationship intelligence helps firms uncover who knows whom, strengthen client engagement, and support more strategic, coordinated outreach across the firm.

According to Laura, "One of the most important things women can do to help themselves with business development is to position their outreach within the context of the various relationships a firm may have with a company and what matters the firm has handled that may be related to the potential client." Using a solid CRM that integrates with the firm's financial systems and has automation and AI built in, can do that.

Another piece of technology that can be vital to promote a business and is also an enterprise solution is Passle. Passle is a legal marketing platform designed to help professionals, including women lawyers, establish and enhance their personal brands through thought leadership. By simplifying the content creation process, and suggesting and helping lawyers write LinkedIn posts, Passle enables lawyers to share their expertise and insights effectively, fostering greater visibility and credibility in their own personal niche. James Barclay, CEO of Passle points out, "For women lawyers in particular, thought leadership is a game-changer. It's an opportunity to lead the conversation without the pressures that go with playing golf or using traditional means of driving business that may feel uncomfortable." According to James, "Thought leadership isn't just a content strategy—it's the fuel to the engine of an attorney's business development efforts. For women, it offers a path to visibility and influence without needing to conform to outdated networking norms."

By working with enterprise systems such as CRMs and experience management systems, and content management systems, firms can provide ways of scaling and igniting individual marketing efforts. Lawyers can use these tools along with a firm's community-driven initiatives to build a robust online presence, connect with peers, and further their positioning as thought leaders.

Rainmaking with Your Marketing Department

Ursula Ben-Hammou is a corporate attorney who decided after fifteen years of practicing that she wanted to follow her passion and work in the marketing department of a law firm. Today, she is based in Mexico as the Latin America business development and marketing leader for Cuatrecasas, an international law firm firmly established in Spain, Portugal and Latin America. Ursula strongly believes rainmaking is not innate—rather, it can and should be taught. It should start early, even at university level, and evolve with each lawyer's style.

"If we started when we were younger, it would be easier. You have years to think and build your personal brand and network."

She emphasizes that lawyers don't need to follow a prescribed business development path—they just need clarity on what they bring to the table.

"Do you know the places you need to be seen? Are you a thought leader? Do you have an online presence?" She urges lawyers to work closely with their business development departments to build a strategy and follow up consistently, and above all, to be authentic in doing so.

Law firms that make intentional, sustained investments in the business development success of women lawyers aren't just doing the right thing—they're making a smart business decision.

From tailored training and thoughtful mentorship to technology tools and leadership pipelines, it's clear that firms can succeed by providing the right support to women lawyers, helping them—and their firms—thrive.

Rainmaking is not a mystery, nor is it reserved for a select few. However, as the global women rainmakers spotlighted here prove, success in rainmaking comes ultimately from within. However, with the right infrastructure, culture, and commitment, every lawyer can be empowered to grow relationships, generate business, and lead with confidence.

Think Piece

How Law Firms Can Play a Role in Helping Women (and Others) Develop Business

By Toni Jaeger-Fine*

When I practiced law from the mid-1980s to the early 1990s, I never heard anyone speak about business development. This likely reflected certain features of law practice at the time, including the absence of meaningful competition and the fact that there was no expectation that junior or even mid-level associates would take part in the business of the firm.

Times have changed. In particular, competition for legal services has exploded, a development that has led law firms to embrace business development as a key strategic imperative.

Unfortunately, women and lawyers from other historically under-represented groups often fall behind when it comes to business development, reinforcing systemic inequities in the ranks of partners and law firm leaders. With women now accounting for a majority of law school graduates in the U.S. (and elsewhere), law firms need to ensure that their female attorneys are empowered to cultivate business.

In the decades since I left the practice of law I have worked with hundreds of attorneys, many of them women, and have had the opportunity to learn of their challenges. I also have been involved in executive education programs through which I have learned from experts in business development, including Deborah Farone. Based on these experiences, I believe that there is much more that law

* Toni Jaeger-Fine is Senior Counselor at Fordham Law School, where she was an assistant dean for more than fifteen years, and Principal of Jaeger-Fine Consulting. She is the author of numerous articles and books, including *Becoming a Lawyer: Discovering and Defining Your Professional Persona* (2d ed. 2023).

firms can do to accelerate business development by their women attorneys.

Create a Strong Culture of Business Development

All law firms seem to *want* a culture that promotes business development, but many fall short when it comes to actually creating and nurturing such a culture.

Communication about the importance of business development is a necessary starting point, but firms must substantiate their words with meaningful action. Firms need to be transparent in establishing expectations and metrics to measure and track business development activities and mechanisms for rewarding attorneys who succeed. Origination and other forms of credit must be allocated fairly—I have heard far too many stories of women cultivating relationships and bringing clients or matters to the firm only to have the credit go to someone else.

Training is also essential and it must address the multiple forms that business development can take. Many law firms seem to take a one-size-fits all approach, but business development training should be more tailored and reinforce that business development is a highly individualized endeavor. Women are often discouraged from assertive business development because "salesmanship" is thought to be too aggressive and unbecoming. But women often have superpowers with great currency for business development, including social and emotional intelligence and the ability to collaborate deeply. Trainings should help them recognize, strengthen, and leverage these abilities.

Coaching by client development professionals and rainmakers should supplement formal trainings, and law firms should include business development efforts as part of their formal and informal feedback processes, providing tailored, actionable feedback tied to individual strengths and goals.

This culture of business development should be inculcated early on in an associate's career. I am baffled by the notion that business development training traditionally begins at the senior associate level, with the expectation that in the few years before they are considered for partnership attorneys can demonstrate their business development potential. To the contrary, successful business development requires a complex skill set that should be nurtured over years—starting with entry-level associates.

Enable Strategic Networking

Engaging successfully in business development activities requires strategic networking. Firms can help their women attorneys identify external networking opportunities that align with their individual practice area/industry, strengths, and interests and that can help them build new and strengthen existing networks.

Internal networking is equally important. Internal networks foster mentoring and sponsorships. Women associates need to connect to those in positions of power, often men—which also reduces the disproportionate burden senior women often experience when it comes to nurturing more junior talent. Internal networking is also crucial to successful cross-servicing, which requires that attorneys know and trust their colleagues and understand intimately the work that they do.

Ensure Client Visibility

Women lawyers should be given client-facing roles and access to prospective clients. Partners should bring female associates to client meetings and pitches and, in due course, ensure that they active contributors rather than mere observers. Women associates ultimately should be involved in relationship management and billing leadership.

Women associates also should be encouraged to get to know in-house counterparts and create a "zipper" relationship with representatives of the client at their own level to further solidify the relationship between client and law firm. Law firms also can facilitate secondments, which help develop an associate's understanding of client needs and internal operations and enable her to build deeper client relationships.

Provide Opportunities for Professional Development

Law firms should be intentional about ensuring that all attorneys have equivalent opportunities to develop their skills and demonstrate their value through stretch assignments and access to tasks that equip them with the tools necessary for long-term success in their practice areas. Housekeeping assignments should be apportioned fairly; many women report that they do a disproportionate amount of this kind of work even when there are more junior male associates on the team—a phenomenon I myself have experienced more times than I can count.

Facilitate Thought Leadership

Law firms can help guide their attorneys toward thought leadership, which can translate directly or indirectly into potential clients. Law firm marketing and client relationship departments can help women (and other) attorneys develop ideas and facilitate connections to media outlets. More established lawyers should be encouraged to collaborate with younger female colleagues by co-authoring pieces and helping them secure invitations to participate in panels or on bar association committees.

* * * *

Ultimately, the responsibility for business development rests with each attorney, but law firms have a pivotal role in removing structural barriers and equipping all attorneys with the tools to succeed.

Postscript

Much of the material for this book was developed in 2024. It was a time I spent living at my desk on Zoom. It was there I conducted sixty interviews with profoundly brilliant and inspiring lawyers, academics, consultants and leaders in the profession. It was also a period of considering who would be appropriate for the various Think Pieces at the end of each chapter. After each interview, I made certain that my notes from the conversation were organized and properly transcribed. It became part of a ritual—finish the interview, organize my notes, and then pick up the phone to call my ninety-two-year-old mother.

My mom, Phyllis Brightman, was a joyful and incredibly social person, with a magnetic personality. I have never met anyone who had so many friends: friends from her days as a realtor, and others she met from collecting antiques, memberships in book clubs or her treasured civic groups. In later years she was an avid bridge player and the center of a whole new social circle, living independently in New Jersey.

During our post-interview call, she would always ask what I was working on and wanted to know who I had spoken with for the book. When I told her about the women I was interviewing and the incredible stories I was hearing, she was elated. She wanted to know everything—how I knew them and, if they were a new contact, how did I make the connection to them. She wanted to know how they achieved their success, and what I learned from each one of them. She loved the fact that on one day I was speaking with someone in Botswana, and on the next day, Italy, France or Singapore. She was fascinated by every nuance I reported of the conversations and every connection.

Only later did I realize how meaningful that curiosity was. My mom had a deep and genuine interest in people and what made them tick. As a schoolteacher in her twenties, she cared deeply for her students. I recently found a note from the 1950s in which she wrote about students that she felt had great promise for the future. Later, as a young parent, she wanted to know not only what books we were reading in elementary school but also demanded to know that they were unbiased and told the real history, the good and the bad, of our country.

And as a realtor, she truly shined. She may have been my first role model in sales—not because she was selling, but because she genuinely cared about the well-being and happiness of her clients.

She took a personal interest in each one and their families. She stayed in touch with them long after the closing of the sale, sending handwritten notes and remembering their wedding anniversaries. It wasn't strategic or calculated. I don't think she even used a calendar to remind herself. It just came naturally to her.

So many of the lessons my mom taught me—about people, relationships, listening, and generosity—are woven into this book. She was an inspiration.

In November of 2024, my mom passed away suddenly. Her loss brought everything to a halt. For a time, I set the book aside. But about a month later, I returned to it. I knew she would have wanted me to finish it and meet my contract's deadline. In fact, she made me promise I'd write another book down the road—a children's book—about the animals living in my backyard. I'd occasionally tell her stories about Gary the Groundhog, and Mrs. Katz, the feline who made an appearance at my doorstep each summer. I promise I'll get to it. But for now, I'm grateful I finished this one.

I hope you enjoyed the book as much as I enjoyed creating it. And I hope, like my mom hoped for me, you find ways to build relationships and to inspire others to do the same.

Index

A

B

C

D

E

F

G

H

I

J

K

L

M

N

O

P

R

S

T

U

V

W

Z

www.ingramcontent.com/pod-product-compliance
Lightning Source LLC
LaVergne TN
LVHW052314200926
848481LV00002B/564

* 9 7 8 1 4 0 2 4 4 9 5 1 2 *